Delaware
CURIOSITIES

Help Us Keep This Guide Up to Date

Every effort has been made by the author and editors to make this guide as accurate
and useful as possible. However, many things can change after a guide is published—
establishments close, phone numbers change, hiking trails are rerouted, facilities come
under new management, etc.

We would love to hear from you concerning your experiences with this guide and how
you feel it could be made better and be kept up to date. While we may not be able to
respond to all comments and suggestions, we'll take them to heart and we'll also make
certain to share them with the author. Please send your comments and suggestions to
the following address:

The Globe Pequot Press
Reader Response/Editorial Department
P.O. Box 480
Guilford, CT 06437

Or you may e-mail us at:

editorial@GlobePequot.com

Thanks for your input, and happy travels!

Delaware CURIOSITIES

QUIRKY CHARACTERS, ROADSIDE ODDITIES & OTHER OFFBEAT STUFF

BETH RUBIN

INSIDERS' GUIDE®

GUILFORD, CONNECTICUT
AN IMPRINT OF THE GLOBE PEQUOT PRESS

The prices, rates, and hours listed in this guidebook were confirmed at press time. We recommend, however, that you call establishments to obtain current information before traveling.

INSIDERS' GUIDE®

Text design by Nancy Freeborn
Layout by Debbie Nicolais
Maps by Rusty Nelson © Morris Book Publishing, LLC
Photo credits: p. 19 Courtesy of Fort Delaware Society; p. 25 Robert T. Zappalorti, Nature's Film and Photo Images; p. 26 John J. Bain; p. 36 Winterthur; pp. 40, 42, 54, 159 Mac Bogert; p. 52, 58 Kent County Tourism; p. 61 Jim Yurasek; p. 63 Courtesy of Biggs Museum of American Art; p. 70 Eric Crossan for Kent County Tourism; p. 87 World Championship Punkin Chunkin; p. 99 Delmarva Poultry Industry, Inc.; p. 97 Long Meadow Farm; p. 112 Art by Richard C. Clifton; p. 121 Marc Clery for Dogfish Head Craft Brewery; p. 128 Ruslana Lambert/Coastal Point; p. 135 Praveen G. Mutalik. All other photos are by the author.

Library of Congress Cataloging-in-Publication Data is available.
ISBN: 978-0-7627-4335-3

Manufactured in the United States of America
First Edition/First Printing

To the wonderful people of Delaware.

DELAWARE

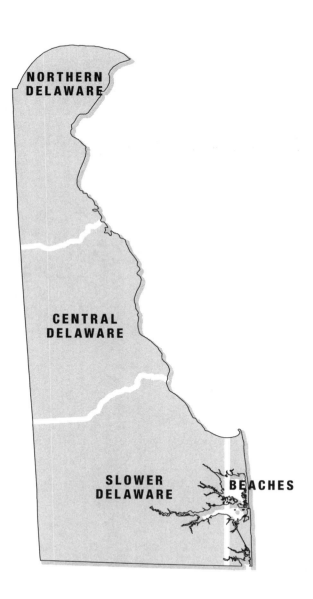

NORTHERN
DELAWARE

CENTRAL
DELAWARE

SLOWER
DELAWARE

BEACHES

Contents

Acknowledgments

Nobody births a book alone. Hate to burst your bubble, but writing ain't no Immaculate Conception. I owe thanks to many people. First, Christine Serio for recommending me for the project, and Mike Urban and The Globe Pequot Press for the opportunity. Working on this was as close to fun as I have had while working. In crisscrossing the state—a feat that can be accomplished in about fifteen minutes—I met many wonderful Delawareans. Without exception, they were friendly, helpful, and, best of all, far from dull. Every road trip was an adventure. I never knew what I'd find, and the photo ops were endless. Even the times I nearly got killed—Mack trucks and SUVs whizzing by as I skidded onto the shoulder to snap a particularly attractive cow or chicken—were worth it.

To Lyn Lewis at the Wilmington CVB; Michele Robinette, Kent County Tourism CVB; Karen Falk, Southern Delaware Tourism; and Carrie Townsend, unofficial goodwill ambassador who introduced me to many of the First State's delights, go special thanks. I couldn't have done it without your help, ladies.

For their assistance, I am grateful to the Delaware Economic Development Office; Historical Society of Delaware; Winterthur staff; Ryan Grover and Sandy Conner at the Biggs Museum of American Art; Connie Parvis at the Delmarva Poultry Industry, Inc.; Jack Shattuck; and everyone else who stopped what they were doing to answer questions and show me around their homes, businesses, museums, and attics.

To my family and friends, thanks, as always, for your encouragement and for supplying me with chocolate PRN. I could go on and on, but I have road fatigue. And I want you to read the book. I hope you get as much pleasure from discovering Delaware's curiosities as I did writing about them.

Introduction

Delaware at a Glance. (A glance is all you get. Blink and you'll cross into Maryland or Pennsylvania.)

Up front I must confess—mea culpa, mea culpa—that, before I got to know it, I assumed Delaware must be a mistake. A little mistake, but a mistake nonetheless. It couldn't possibly be worthy of exploration, I mused. First off, I didn't know a soul who lived there, so right away it was suspect. And it had a funny shape. Hailing from exit 142A in the Garden State (no. 46 in area), I thought Delaware too small (no. 49) and too dull to merit exploration. What a dunce!

I've learned a lot since I stopped to take a closer look in the 1960s. Over the years I've schmoozed with the natives, gone down less-traveled roads, and attended more than my share of odd events. I can tell you, unequivocally, there is no shortage of curiosities in the First State. You can say that again! There is no shortage of curiosities in the First State.

Festivals don't get any hokier than Bridgeville's annual Punkin Chunkin, where locals hurl their leftover Halloween squash from home-made catapults. For prizes yet!

In Millsboro, Judy and Lou Hagen craft whimsical metal sculptures in their garage studio October through April. The rest of the year, they haul produce in their eighteen-wheel rig and search for scrap metal with artistic potential.

Each spring on the full moon, voyeurs congregate on Delaware Bay beaches to watch horsehoe crabs get it on (with or without Barry White). You thought a ménage à trois was wild? Sometimes you can't count the participants in this bacchanale.

The second-smallest state after Rhode Island, Delaware was first to ratify the U.S. Consititution. "That was a good thing," as Mel Brooks might say. But where did the state's name come from? The good news: It did not derive from the god-awful 1950s pop tune sung by Perry

Delaware CURIOSITIES

Como, a barber turned crooner from faraway Ohio. Nope. Instead, historians credit Thomas West ("Tom" or "Tommy" to his intimates), the Third Baron De La Warr. Classy name, eh? Mr. (or is it Mr. Baron Sir?) De La Warr was no trailer trash. The first governor of the Virginia Colony was an Oxford-educated Brit who kept his head when acquitted of charges that he'd plotted with Lord Essex to off Queen Elizabeth I. I'm not sure what that has to do with chemicals, corporations, and cheesesteaks, but you gotta admit it's mildly interesting.

Last count, Delaware had about 841,000 people, less than the city of San Jose, California. After the Labor Day exodus from the beaches, the population dwindles to 59, give or take a few. Delaware spreads north to south throughout three counties: New Castle, Kent, and Sussex. (Speaking of spread, think of Kent as the lox and cream cheese; New Castle and Sussex as the bagel halves.)

Put your pedal to the metal, and you can drive from northernmost New Castle County south to the Maryland border in under three hours. Heck, the state is only 97 miles long and 37 miles wide. Get up early, and you can see it all before lunch! A scintillating car game is to count the chicken houses or flattened skunks you drive over (or smell). Bet you can't count that high. Just joshing . . . sort of.

The curious state line between Delaware and Pennsylvania is the only arc serving as a geophysical boundary in the entire country. Extending 12 miles from the New Castle Court House cupola, it's known as the Twelve-Mile Circle. Well, I guess so: They wouldn't call it Eleven or Thirteen, would they? I can't help wondering what was so magical about the number twelve. But I'll save that for another book. Maybe.

Did you know that Delaware hosted the Walt Disney Company a couple of years ago? Why are you surprised? Delaware is, after all, the "corporate capital of the world." Mickey Mouse execs filled Georgetown's historic Court of Chancery for a trial whose roots, some say, were planted in Fantasyland. At night they bedded down at the Bellmoor Inn in Rehoboth Beach, a town with a large gay population that was once the site of Methodist camp meetings. Go figure.

Some other curious Delaware stuff you may not know (and could probably live without): Delaware was the last state to receive an official NPS (National Park Service) unit. If anyone knows why, please write to me. Meanwhile, Cape Henlopen State Park is as good as any ole national park in my book. And this is my book. So there.

Delaware was the last state to use the "hundreds" geographical division. There are thirty-three of them, and they're used in property tax assessments. Credit William Penn for bringing this quaint Brit practice that settlements should be divided into sections of one hundred families each. Get it? For the number-impaired, a hundred is about the size of a township.

Delaware is also known as the Diamond State. Thank you, Thomas Jefferson, who observed that, like the diamond, the state was small but important.

With no less than Eve and Adam as a prototype, Delaware was carved from Pennsylvania. Originally known as the "Three Lower Counties" along Delaware Bay, it morphed into the Delaware Colony.

The state insect is the ladybug (except in July and August, when mosquitoes reign by divine rule and ladybugs flee to Maine, where it's cooler).

The biggest industries are chickens and tourists (and the occasional chicken tourist or touristy chicken).

The average size of a Delaware farm is 235 acres.

Delaware supports seven breweries. Despite a thriving dairy industry, suds win over milk every time. But you already knew that.

Would you believe Delaware has fifteen golf courses? That's a lot of sand traps and nineteenth holes for such a tiny state. Credit (or discredit) the influx of retirees.

In my purely subjective poll, the state's most popular foods are: chicken, seafood, hamburgers, pizza, and hoagies/subs/grinders. Call these belly busters what you will, Delawareans love their scrumptious, cholesterol-laden, calorie-packed meals on an elongated bun. The bigger, the better.

But, contrary to what you may believe, bigger is not always better. As a visitor, you'll find that "good things come in small packages." And packed into Delaware's scant 2,500 square miles is a wealth of curiosities. Don't take my word for it. Grab this book (after you pay for it) and go see for yourself.

DELAWARE (WHAT DID DELA-WARE?)

Oh what did Dela-ware boy
What did Dela-ware
What did Dela-ware boy
What did Dela-ware
She wore a brand New Jersey,
She wore a brand New Jersey,
She wore a brand New Jersey,
That's what she did wear

One, two, three, four

Oh, why did Cali-fon-ia
Why did Cali-fon
Why did Cali-fon-ia
Was she all alone
She called to say Ha-wa-ya
She called to say Ha-wa-ya
She called to say Ha-wa-ya
That's why she did call

Uno, deis, tre, quatro

Oh what did Missi-sip boy
What did Missi-sip
What did Missi-sip boy
Through her pretty lips

She sipped a Minne-sota
She sipped a Minne-sota
She sipped a Minne-sota
That's what she did sip

Where has Ore-gon boy
Where has Ore-gon
If you wan Al-ask-a
Go ahead and ask her
She went to pay her Texas
She went to pay her Texas
She went to pay her Texas

That's where she has gone
Well how did Wis-con-sin boy
She stole a New-brass-key
Too bad that Arkan-saw boy
And so did Tenne-see
It made poor Flori-di boy
It made poor Flori-di, you see
She died in Miss-our-i boy
She died in Miss-our-i

Oh what did Dela-ware boy
What did Dela-ware . . .

Sometimes smaller is better.

Irving Gordon, a Brooklyn-born composer and lyricist, wrote the punny song. Recorded by Perry Como in 1959, it rose to number 22 on the Billboard charts. Some say it did better in Great Britain and hit number 3. I'm from Missouri on that. Meanwhile, Gordon made a name for himself composing movie soundtracks and an early folk song, "Allentown Jail." To my knowledge he never stepped foot in Delaware. *Quel dommage.*

But was this the state's official song? Nope. The official song is "Our Delaware," written by George B. Hynson and composed by M.S. Brown, but you'll find very few Delawareans who actually know the words.

NORTHERN DELAWARE

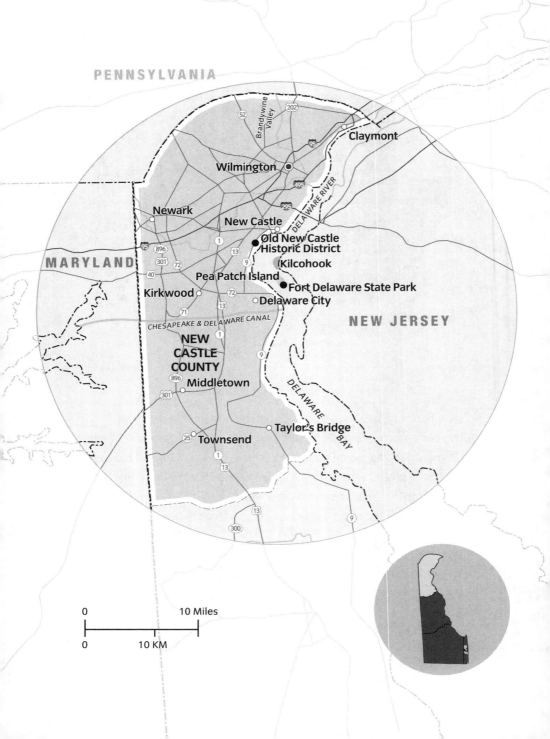

PENNSYLVANIA

Brandywine Valley

52

202

95

Claymont

Wilmington

495

295

DELAWARE RIVER

Newark

New Castle

1

Old New Castle
Historic District

Kilcohook

MARYLAND

896

13

9

301

72

Fort Delaware State Park

40

Pea Patch Island

72

Delaware City

Kirkwood

13

NEW JERSEY

71

CHESAPEAKE & DELAWARE CANAL

NEW
CASTLE
COUNTY

9

896

Middletown

301

DELAWARE BAY

25

Taylor's Bridge

Townsend

1

13

13

300

9

0   10 Miles

0   10 KM

NORTHERN DELAWARE

New Castle County

Resembling a crooked finger pointing at south Jersey's rump, New Castle County is where you land after crossing the Delaware Bay Bridge from the Garden State. Delaware's most heavily populated county has half a million people. Rumor has it that most skedaddled over the bridge when New Jersey ran out of room.

The scenic Chateau Country of hills and forests bordering Pennsylvania in the northern part of the county is where the Du Pont clan chose to settle, long before Tyvek wrapped every new house in the U. S. of A. As you head south from DuPontville, the hills flatten and the forests give way to farmland, tidal marshes, and industry. Wilmington, the largest and best-known city, is the state's commercial, financial, and cultural heart. Newark—that's *New-ark,* not *Newrk* (dropped vowel)—is home to the University of Delaware and the Fightin' Blue Hens.

The city of New Castle has a split personality—part old, part new; part commercial, part historic. New Castle is home to Mike's Harley-Davidson, whose sign, on a clear day, is visible from the San Fernando Valley. On the former site of a Howard Johnson's motel, Mike's is the largest H-D dealer in the country. Leaving sticker shock for culture shock, one can revisit the past in Old New Castle—all the way back to when the state was a colony. Old New Castle perches on choice riverfront property. (Location, location, location!)

Delaware City (hardly a city, as its population hovers around 1,400) stands near the Delaware Bay entrance to the C & D Canal. It's also the departure point for Pea Patch Island and Fort Delaware, site of a former Civil War prison—a nice place to visit, but you wouldn't want to live there.

Oh My Darley, Oh My Darley
Claymont

Felix O. (Octavius) C. (Carr) Darley (1821–1888) may not be a household name, at least in your household, but this world-renowned illustrator lived for many years in Claymont, in Delaware's far northeastern corner—any closer to the Pennsylvania border and you'd need a passport. Among Darley's contributions to the art world were illustrations for books by Irving (author Washington Irving, not deli owner Irving Katz), Poe, Hawthorne, Dickens, and Cooper. Not a bad lot to hang out with. He's probably best known among the literati for his illustrations for James Fenimore Cooper's "The Legend of Sleepy Hollow" and Washington Irving's "Rip Van Winkle." In fact, he illustrated all thirty-two of Cooper's novels.

If you're passing through on your way to Philly, D.C., New York, Newfoundland, or Tierra del Fuego, stop at the Darley House at the intersection of the old Philadelphia Pike (U.S. Highway 13) and Darley Road (you were expecting Piscataway Boulevard?) to pay your respects. In 1863 Darley purchased the late eighteenth-century house, naming it "The Wren's Nest"; it's said he used to call his wife "my little wren." But we have to wonder why he didn't call it "The Crow's Nest" or "The Well-Feathered Nest." History has always presented us with more than its share of mysteries. This is one of them.

Darley lived and worked here, overseeing additions and renovations between illustrations, until his death in 1888. The house has been on the National Register of Historic Places since 1974. When he died Darley was completing a Dickens portfolio. Dickens himself spent two weeks here in 1867 during his American tour. (No reports on whether he was a good houseguest or remembered to send a thank-you note.)

Today it is a private residence, but you can find more information at www.FOCDarley.org.

SOME FACTS ABOUT CLAYMONT

Before bidding *adieu* to Darley and Claymont, here are some interesting factoids to dish at your next dinner party:

The town was once a summertime destination for wealthy Philadelphians.

Financier J. J. Raskob (Empire State Building and General Motors—not too shabby) planned Al Smith's presidential campaign from his Claymont home with . . . Go on, take a guess . . . Give up? Joseph Kennedy Sr.

Actress Valerie Bertinelli was born here on April 23, 1960. You may remember her as Barbara Cooper in *One Day at a Time*, numerous forgettable film and TV roles, and as the ex-wife of Eddie Van Halen.

A Canal Runs Through It
Delaware City

The 14-mile C & D (Chesapeake and Delaware) Canal cuts a swath west-to-east (or east-to-west, if you prefer) through Maryland and Delaware, connecting the Chesapeake Bay at Chesapeake City, Maryland, to Delaware Bay south of Delaware City. Of the many commercial U.S. canals built in the nineteenth century, it's the only one still in use.

Talk about shortcuts! If not for the canal, commercial vessels (and countless recreational boaters) on the Chesapeake would have to go all the way around the Delmarva peninsula or south to Norfolk for access to the Atlantic Ocean. The canal shortens by some 300 miles the route between Baltimore and Philadelphia—and farther afield, other northeast cities and Europe.

When it opened in 1829, mules and horses towed the barges and sailing ships through four locks. The U.S. Army Corps of Engineers took over in the 1920s, dredging the channel to a more hospitable depth of 12 feet and width of 90. Today, after subsequent refinements, it's 35 feet deep and 450 feet wide—enough for two oceangoing ships to pass each other and not go bump in the night. Or day. You may not have reason to navigate through the locks, but you can enjoy driving over the many scenic bridges or biking along the shore. Log on to www
.pennways.org for details.

I'll Take Fries with That

Newark

In a state known more for its chicken, pizza, and subs, Jake's has earned well a niche for primo hamburgers. No less an authority than Holly Eats (www.hollyeats.com) has rated Jake's four (excellent) grease stains out of a possible five (outstanding). It doesn't get much better than that in burgerland—especially in Delaware, where Blue Hens and Perdue chickens dominate.

The original location in Newark (1100 Ogleton Road; 302–737–1118; www.jakeshamburgers.com) opened to little fanfare in 1991. In short order aficionados were lining up for their cheeseburger deluxes. What sets Jake's apart? The meat is *fresh* (never frozen), and the burgers are grilled. Also, the

Jake's fans chow down.

prices are like Delaware chicks—*cheap, cheap, cheap* ($2.30 for a hamburger with the works). Jake's cooks with cholesterol-free oil; that means no trans fats. If like New York, Delaware institutes a statewide ban on the culprit, Jake's can shrug and get on with business as usual. Run your own tests if you wish. I'll take Jake's word.

I'll also take chili and/or cheese on my fries when I'm feeling unusually perverse, and I urge you to do the same. Wipe the sneer off your face—don't knock it if you haven't tried it. Unadorned, the potatoes are crunchy and tasty for purists. Go ahead, have 'em your way. It's a win-win situation. And the shakes and malts? Mmm mmm, thick and creamy; made with hand-dipped ice cream, not frozen air.

Good news for us burger lovers—Jake's has four other Delaware locations and is expanding into other states. I'm thinking of taking the huge advance for doing this book and opening my own franchise. You read it here first!

Waltz to Matilda's
Newark

In a unique eatery near the Fightin' Blue Hens of the University of Delaware, fowl isn't the only thing on the menu. Waltz over to Matilda's Pub & Barbie (801 South College Avenue; 302–737–4800; www.matildas restaurant.com), where Aussie (pronounced *ozzie*) owner Lee Buzalek presides over one of only four Australian restaurants in the United States. "Actually," he says, "the other three—in Seattle, New York, and somewhere in the Midwest—are bars, too, so we're the only pure Australian restaurant." Stick that in your diggery-doo!

Born in Adelaide, Lee spent time in Sydney before moving to the States in 1977, persuaded by his American wife, a teacher he had met in Sydney. "She wanted to come home," he shrugs. A loving and dutiful bloke, he followed. His first job, making pizza at a Shakey's in Newark, was followed by stints as a car salesman, Radio Shack manager, and owner of a computer shop for twenty years. "I'm an entrepreneur at heart," Lee says. Who's to argue?

As for Matilda's, according to Lee, "Everything is fresh. Nothing is prepackaged—nothing." The personal touch is everywhere. The menu features Wagga Wagga (pronounced *wogga*) Nachos, named for the small town in Victoria where he did his basic training in the Australian army; beef pies ("sausage rolls like your hot dogs, eaten at Australian football games—very traditional"); XXXX (spicy) Chook Strips ("colloquial for chicken"); barramundi ("good game fish from the Northern Territory, similar to freshwater bass in texture and taste"); and kangaroo, seasoned with Aussie spices and pan-fried. The Roo Burger and Aussie Burger are hits, along with the Tasmanian Spaghetti. For the less adventurous, the menu lists steaks, lamb, chicken, seafood, and salads.

How's the food? As they say Down Under, "Ace."

Watch Your Head
Newark

If you think the rotisserie chicken and mac and cheese served up at the Boston Market at College Avenue (Route 896) and Welsh Tract Church Road couldn't possibly have any relation to local history, think again. Clean your plate, then head down Welsh Tract Church Road to the little brick congregation established by Welsh settlers in 1703.

The Revolutionary War's Battle of Cooch's Bridge, the only battle of the war fought on Delaware turf, took place roughly between the restaurant and the church. The colonials fighting that battle on September 3, 1777, used their heads, shielding themselves from British rifle fire behind the church's stone walls. One lad, Charlie Miller, bobbed

WHY THOSE HENS ARE BLUE

Delaware's official state bird is the blue hen, excuse me, Blue Hen. Around here you show a Blue Hen r-e-s-p-e-c-t. Not surprisingly, the Fightin' Blue Hen is the University of Delaware's mascot, and the jocks are referred to as Blue Hens. (Last time I checked, professors were still professors.) So what's the significance of blue hens? Why not red roosters? Or speckled guinea fowl? The origin sounds like pure folklore, but historians claim it's true. Who cares? It's a nice story, so read on.

During the Revolutionary War, one Captain Jonathan Caldwell had a reputation for marching to his own drummer. He gave chickens to the men in his company instead of rabbits' feet or four-leaf clovers for good luck. (Huh? They didn't have enough trouble schlepping backpacks, muskets, and drums in all kinds of weather? They needed a chicken as a talisman?) It appears there was a method to Caldwell's madness. The chickens were said to be descendants of famous Blue Hens, known for their combativeness. Get it?

Between battles the men entertained themselves—and picked up some spare change—by staging cockfights between the Blue Hens. Nice little money-making operation. No paper trail. No tax ramifications. Word scattered faster than chicken feathers. Quick as you could ask, "Why did the blue hens cross the battlefield?", the soldiers' bravery was compared to that of the fighting cocks.

Fast forward to April 14, 1939, when the Blue Hen was officially declared the state bird. And now, as Paul Harvey would say, you know the rest of the story.

when he should have weaved and had a bit of bad luck: His head got in the line of fire. Oops. Historians say the cannonball took his head clean off before tearing into the church. Look closely and you can see where the cannonball damage was repaired after the unfortunate incident.

But Charlie didn't get mad, he got even. Several reports told of subsequent attacks by a headless horseman who chopped off British heads before roaring off on his steed. And that's how Charlie Miller gained fame as the Headless Horseman of Welsh Tract Road.

Which Came First?
Newark

According to William H. Williams, retired University of Delaware professor of history and the author of *Delmarva's Chicken Industry: 75 Years of Progress,* the egg came before the chicken. He ought to know. Williams interviewed thirty-five individuals on tape and talked to a couple dozen off the record (and who knows how many chickens) for his five-chapter opus chronicling the industry from its earliest days.

Williams says that in the early 1900s, the idea of selling edible chickens was an afterthought—a P.S., if you will, to egg production. Back then people ate young male chickens (cockerels) and old hens who hadn't laid anything, much less an egg, in eons. What feathered the nests of local farmers, according to Williams, was eggs, which farmers' wives traded for store merchandise or sold to food brokers in the cities.

In one anecdotal entry, Williams tells of Arthur Perdue, a Salisbury, Maryland, railroad agent who connected the dots between egg-laying and profitability. In 1920 he said ta-ta to the railroad and started a commercial egg farm. If the name sounds familiar, that's probably due to Arthur's son, Frank, who left Salisbury College in 1939 to work for his dad, succeeded him as president, and turned the company into one of the largest poultry processors in the country. Frank Perdue's folksy ads helped to drive annual sales from $56 million in 1970 to $1.2 billion in 1991.

If you want to learn more, the book is available at the University of Delaware bookstore (302–831–2637; www.udel.edu/bookstore).

Amazing Space
New Castle

Amazon.com's New Castle fulfillment center—a fancy name for a gargantuan warehouse—is approximately *200,000* square feet. Consider this: A football field (including the end zones) is 57,600 square feet, or about one acre. Phew! We're talkin' close to four acres of books, electronics, and Tickle Me Elmos.

And it's not like the New Castle facility, which opened in 1997, is the only one in the United States. Nope, it is but one of twelve nationwide. According to a normal-size Amazon executive (free shipping included if you purchase two), "I'm afraid we don't disclose volume capacity for any one of our facilities. However, on our busiest day in 2006, Amazon .com's worldwide facilities shipped more than *2.7 million* units in a single day."

I don't know about you, but I fantasize about spending a few hours in one of these fulfillment centers, fulfilling myself with a shopping cart the size of Lake Michigan. Unfortunately, Amazon sees otherwise: The facility is not open to the general public. Wait a sec, I'm no general, never served in the military. If you're hankering to see how your orders are processed, Amazon does open its doors on occasion for tours "in conjunction with local universities." Maybe if you matriculate at the University of Delaware as a business student, you can penetrate the walls of this fortress—but I'm not sure that a look-see is worth the price of admission.

Easy Rider Mike Schwartz
New Castle

You gotta hand it to Mike Schwartz. In 1994 the University of Delaware grad and owner of two profitable businesses bought a Wilmington Harley-Davidson dealership on the skids. By revving up customer service, Schwartz quadrupled sales in the first year.

Fast forward to today. A few miles from Wilmington in New Castle, hog lovers and wannabes detour off one of the East Coast's busiest traffic corridors to Mike's Famous Harley-Davidson (2160 New Castle Avenue; 800–FAMOUS–HD; www.mikesfamous.com).

So many bikes, so little time.

The orange and black sign, visible for miles, beckons travelers from the blacktop just south of the Delaware Memorial Bridge. More than 100,000 cars a day burn rubber on this portion of Interstate 295, passing Mike's. I'm no marketing maven, but I'd say that's a fair-size audience.

While other entrepreneurs "took paradise and put up a parking lot," in 1996 Mike bought just under six acres of New Castle decrepitude that used to be a Howard Johnson Motor Lodge and turned it into a tourist mecca. The original HoJo registration hut, with its low-slung pagoda– style roof, serves as on-site offices for Mike's support staff. Drop in at the 40,000-square-foot showroom any day of the week and sidle down rows of gleaming machines—Electra Glides, Roadsters, Super Glides, Low Riders, Softails, Fat Boys. Every time a Harley is sold, a bell clangs and employees drop what they're doing to exchange high fives.

The showroom may be the top attraction for most visitors, but there's more than what meets the denim-clad rear. The warehouse- themed restaurant, done in wheel and conveyor belt decor, serves killer chili (a prize winner in *Delaware* magazine polls) and other tasty road fare. An adjacent museum grew around the 1972 Harley Wide Glide rid- den around the world by double-amputee Guinness World Record holder Dave Barr.

Not for nothin' did *DealerNews* vote Mike's the #1 Dealer Worldwide. During its first year it produced revenue of $13 million, and in 2005 it revved up to $53 million. *Ka-Ching!*

In case you're wondering, Mike's first Harley, a 1994 FLSTN Heritage, is but a cloud of dust on the highway of life. Today Mike warms the seat of a 2007 Softail Custom. "Like a road trip on a Harley," Mike says, "it's not the destination that's appealing. It's the journey."

Almost Williamsburg
Old New Castle

In the 1930s and 1940s, Daniel Bates led a group of citizens interested in preserving the town of New Castle. They hoped to subsidize their efforts with Rockefeller bucks, like the greenbacks that had poured into Williamsburg. Using the Virginia hot spot as a prototype, the locals formed committees, did studies, hired consultants and architects, traveled to Virginia, researched, met some more, considered plans, discussed the pros and cons, locked horns, talked some more, and enlisted the services of attorneys. You get the picture. You know, like how the federal government operates, but on a smaller scale.

How long do I have to pose like this?

After years of their machinations, the Rockefeller money earmarked for such projects had headed south—literally. The well had dried up. So the town of New Castle ceased and desisted from its vision. But that's OK. In fact, it probably saved New Castle from blatant commercialism and artificiality. IMHO (in my humble opinion), New Castle's diverse architecture (Federal, Georgian, British Colonial, and Victorian), colonial–era history, bricked sidewalks and cobblestone streets, Delaware River setting, and European feel far exceed Williamsburg. And George Washington is said to have attended a wedding reception at the Amstel House. What more could you want? Go see for yourself.

For more information on Old New Castle, call the Historic New Castle Visitors Bureau at (800) 558–1550 or go to www.visitnewcastle history.org.

BORDERLINE

Take a look at Delaware's wacky border with Pennsylvania. If you think a Paul Bunyanesque draftsman knelt down with a huge compass to draw the boundary between the neighboring states, think again. The reason for the arc is tied up with land disputes over the original grants from King Charles II to William Penn.

King Chuck, a thoughtful monarch, didn't want the newly gifted land for Pennsylvania to tick off the Duke of York, whose holdings lay to the south. So Chuck avoided the possible sticky wicket by ruling that the boundary between Delaware and Pennsylvania would extend exactly 12 miles from the cupola of the New Castle Court House. But why 12? Maybe he couldn't count any higher? Or he liked the sound of it? *Twelve.*

Anyway, that's how come an arc separates northern New Castle County from Pennsylvania—the only state boundary of its kind in the United States.

Plenty of curb appeal, but no garage or hot tub.

DELAWARE IS CLOSED

A minor road next to a golf course, Ebright Road crosses the Delaware–Pennsylvania border near U.S. Highway 202 (Concord Pike). In 1963 the popular TV show *Candid Camera* posted a closed sign next to the one reading WELCOME TO DELAWARE. *Candid Camera's* creator and longtime host, Allen Funt, stood by the sign wearing a rented trooper's uniform and a serious expression. When people approached, he pointed to the sign.

The first car pulled up, turned around, and left. Another driver pulled over, got out of his car, and began walking toward the sign. An actor dressed as a highway worker (complete with orange cone, hard hat, and clipboard) offered assistance. The driver asked, "What's going on in Delaware? When do you think it'll reopen? I live there, and my family is in there." One disgruntled motorist asked if he could wait at the barricade until someone left so he could enter the state. A woman asked, "Is Jersey open?"

Unable to maintain his poker face a nanosecond longer, Funt cracked a smile and delivered the signature line, "Smile, you're on *Candid Camera*," ending the taped segment. After the show aired, Funt said it demonstrated "how easily people can be led by any kind of authority figure."

So when will Delaware reopen? Enuf already. I've got family in there.

Keeping out the riff-raff.

NORTHERN DELAWARE

Shake, Rattle, and Boo
Old New Castle

Historic Old New Castle is a happenin' place—and not just for the living. For more than a hundred years, people have reported seeing a woman dressed in blue standing in the windows of the historic Amstel House, home to the New Castle Historical Society, at 2 East Fourth Street. So? Maybe a bored colonial hausfrau was looking for attention. But the word on the cobblestone street is, nobody was home in the Amstel House at the time of the sightings. Some think the figure may have been the ghost of a woman named Elizabeth, whose infant died in the house. Despondent, Elizabeth met her maker soon thereafter. Visitors can view a mourning ring, inscribed by Elizabeth's husband ("I mourn thy virtue lost to me.") during a guided tour.

Another Amstel House resident, Anna Finney, was devastated when her fiancé was killed in 1755. She took to her bed for a spell, then grudgingly gave in to her father's wishes and married a cousin whose last name also happened to be Finney, making her Mrs. Anna Finney Finney. (Which may have pushed her over the edge.) In addition, another Elizabeth is said to have resided in the Amstel House, surviving her husband and two of their three children who succumbed to TB. She was so distraught—*How distraught was she?*—she moved in with her in-laws. Talk about jumping from the frying pan into the fire.

A block away, at the David Finney Inn, 216 Delaware Street (302–322–6367), there is, reputedly, an occasional extra—and nonpaying—guest. Ever since the tavern-turned-inn was built in 1685, some folks have reported a ghost rattling the upstairs windows. Legend also has it that a second ghost used to hang out at the coffee station in the old dining room—now the Chef's Table restaurant. (Maybe the ghost couldn't find a Starbucks or Wawa?) Several years ago, before renovations began on the dining room, a feng shui expert advised the chef to placate the ghost by leaving a cup of coffee. No word as to whether the ghost preferred his joe black or with sugar and cream—or if he even emptied the cup.

Find out more by reserving a spot on the popular Haunted Old New Castle tour held several times every October around *their* favorite holiday. Tours of the Amstel House are given April through December, Wednesday through Sunday. Call (302) 322–2794 or visit www.new castlehistory.org for information on both.

No Peas in This Patch
Pea Patch Island

Smack in the middle of Delaware Bay, between Delaware and New Jersey, lies Pea Patch Island and Fort Delaware State Park. Legend has it that the island got its name when a boat filled with peas went aground on the swampy shores. (Hey, I report the news, I don't make it.) Today you may find some green mold, but few, if any, peas.

The fort protected and defended the Delaware River and the ports of Wilmington and Philadelphia from the War of 1812 through World War II. Fire ravaged the original structures, but you can't keep a good fort down, and it was rebuilt in time for the Civil War. Visitors enjoy tours, hands-on exhibits, reenactments, and other special events throughout the year. I doubt you'd want to spend the night alone in the fort, or even with a good friend. But it's a fascinating place to visit.

Fort Delaware gained notoriety as a prison camp during the Civil War. Think of it as Alcatraz lite—or Gitmo north. Today it's a big tourist draw and an important link to the past. The Fort Delaware Society, most of whose members are descendants of soldiers from the Confederate *and* Union armies, keeps things humming and raises public awareness through research, restoration, and educational projects.

Confederate soldiers began arriving here in July 1861 for what they believed would be, um, short-term imprisonment. (Imagine this scene: "Men, we're going on an outing. Drop the bayonets and muskets; grab your Hawaiian-print shirts, sunscreen, and shades.") According to historians, tourists swarmed to ogle the arriving prisoners.

About 35,000 Rebels called this pentagon fortress home. Some home. There has to be a reason (or reasons) why it was often referred to as the "Andersonville of the North." Many Confederate captives and their Union guards died here. Disease, ill treatment, poor diet, and contaminated water—with not a watering hole other than the bay for miles—took their toll. The ghosts of some of these unfortunate souls are said to inhabit the island still.

Fort Delaware—A nice place to visit but . . .

Also inhabiting the island are birds—lots and lots of birds—so you may want to wear a hat when you visit. The birds are nonpartisan, disclaiming ties to the Blue or the Gray. Pea Patch is home to a large heron rookery and several species of water and wading birds, great egrets and ibises among them. It's been chirped that this is their favorite refueling spot when migrating north and south on the Atlantic Flyway—sort of like how we nonflyers have our favorite highway rest stops.

Interpreters in Civil War–era dress regale visitors with stories of the fort and its inhabitants during tours, and special events and reenactments also take place here. For a chilling experience, I recommend taking a Candlelight Ghost Tour. Tour times and special events vary by season; call (302) 834–7941 or go to www.visitthefort.com for details.

Since it's only a half mile from the mainland to the island, you may be tempted to swim. I urge you not to. The water could be cleaner, and the tankers and muscle boats might mistake you for trash. Ferries depart regularly from the Delaware City dock for the ten-minute ride; call (302) 832–7708 for details. *NOTE:* No food is sold on the island, but you can BYO and snack at one of the picnic tables. If you're lookin' for peas, however, you're out of luck. Take a can with you.

Light by the Side of the Road
Taylor's Bridge

One fine June day I was driving along rural Route 9, aka Taylor's Bridge Road, minding my business, past fields, farmhouses, and double-wides, when what to my wondering eyes should appear— not a miniature sleigh, but a lighthouse! I took my pulse, felt my forehead, and pinched myself. No, I wasn't halluci- nating. Blimey! I'd stumbled on a lighthouse by the side of the road.

I'll smack the next tourist who thinks I'm an oil well!

After a chat with locals, I filled in the blanks. Erected in 1910, the cast-iron Reedy Island Range Rear Light still guides maritime traffic on the Delaware River. By timing the flashes from the lighthouse's DCB-224 aero beacon, the captains of boats cruising local waters can determine their location. A light keeper lived on-site for many years, but electrification squashed that in the 1930s. Light keeper Harry Liston, then keeper of the nearby Liston Range Front Light, south of Port Penn in Bayview, would drive over monthly and replace burned-out lamps. The light keeper's house and outbuildings fell apart from studied neglect, and after automation took over in 1943, Harry got a pink slip.

Word on the street is, vandals set the fire in 2002 that destroyed the two-story, clapboard light keeper's house, outhouse, and brick oil house. Today all that remains are the skeletal structure and what's left of a small barn. Over the years preservationists have made noise about preserving the site, but no one has yet stepped up to the plate.

If you have a GPS in your land yacht, set it for latitude 39.4064, longitude 75.5898. If you're disadvantaged like some of us, head south from Odessa on Highway 13/Dupont Highway for 2 miles. Go east (left) onto Fieldsboro Road and continue for 1.6 miles. Right onto Taylor's Bridge Road (Highway 9) and continue 3 miles to lighthouse.

Where Have All the Oak Trees Gone?

Townsend

There are no nuts like local nuts. In this case, acorns. It comes as no surprise that local acorns take to Delaware soil much better than those from other states. Makes sense to me. So for the past few years, volunteers have gathered acorns from Lums Pond State Park in Bear (New Castle County), Brecknock County Park in Camden (Kent County), and Redden State Forest near Georgetown (Sussex County). They send the acorns to inmates at Sussex Correctional Institute in Slower Delaware. Wait, it gets better! The inmates plant the seeds and monitor their growth into seedlings. When they reach maturity (the seedlings, not the inmates), they're used for statewide reforestation.

The effort came about when huge numbers of Delaware oak trees were felled—to make way for farms, roads, and houses. Some call it progress. For a while acorns were imported from North Carolina and Tennessee. Unfortunately, the acorns balked at the Delaware soil and climate, different from what they were used to. (I also believe they missed the local BBQ in their native states.) So the acorns refused to grow. That's when Delaware's Private Lands Assistance Program stepped in and initiated the acorn-gathering initiative.

It's not just about the trees. Acorns from oaks feed squirrels, chipmunks, turkeys, and deer. When the trees go missing, so do the animals' food sources and, ultimately, the critters themselves.

BOGGED-DOWN TURTLES

State surveyors prepping for construction of proposed U.S. Highway 301 in southern New Castle County got a thumbs-up during the summer of 2006 when, after searching for several months, they failed to unearth any bog turtles. No, this was not the subject of another weird reality show, but it was good news for developers—and the teeny, semiaquatic reptiles (weighing approximately four ounces soaking wet) that are indigenous to the area.

After teams surveyed more than twenty-five wetland areas on four occasions, they came up empty, finding no evidence of the critters that are on the DNREC's (Department of Natural Resources and Environmental Control) list of threatened species under the Endangered Species Act. If they had found the turtles, the developers would have been required to build a bridge over the turtles' habitat or, at least, modify the road's path. (And you thought developers were coldhearted and greedy. Oh ye of little faith!)

Roughly 3 inches long (the length of an average developer's, um, thumb), the bog turtle resembles those that are sold in some pet stores. In case you come across one when you're out hiking, and you can't decide if it's a bog or spotted turtle, look for the identifying yellow or orange mark behind each eye. Most of the year these turtles hibernate in coastal bogs between southern New England and Maryland, but enough is enough when it comes to hibernating, even for bog turtles. Between April and June they break out of the mud to make baby bog turtles.

Think it's easy staying a step ahead of developers?

Despite the surveyors' efforts and findings, area naturalists remain skeptical, citing the turtle's size (or lack thereof) and agility. Some think the turtles may have kept one step ahead of the law and surveyors. A job posting by the state's Endangered Species program for bog turtle surveyors ("prior experience preferred but not necessary") in spring 2006 did little to inspire confidence among environmentalists.

US 301 connects Maryland with Middletown, Delaware, before veering north to U.S. Highway 40. The proposed road would connect with U.S. Highway 1 and Interstate 95 at a cost of approximately $500 million to $700 million. That would buy a lot of turtles.

Ball Snaps Record
Wilmington

In 1998 John Bain of Wilmington finished creating the world's largest rubber-band ball. According to John, it took "eight years to complete, three of which I worked on it almost every day like a part-time job." Five feet tall and weighing in at 3,120 pounds, the ball—not John—has a circumference of 15.1 feet. (Sounds like a guy I went out with. Once.)

John says he was sitting around the mail room of the Wilmington office of Skadden, Arps, Slate, Meagher & Flom LLP and Affiliates, one of the world's largest law firms, when he started fiddling with office supplies to satisfy his artistic side and stave off boredom. Twice a day he'd pick up mail from the post office and cop some rubber bands. (Wonder if his attorney-employers knew about this.) That's when things started to snap.

Pushing rubber bands is exercise enough for John Bain.

NORTHERN DELAWARE

After the ball had tipped the scale at thirty pounds, he began to woo companies with the promise of breaking the world record and sharing with them the publicity. One company bit and started feeding John's habit. About 850,000 bands later, *voila!* He had a 3,120-pound ball that he swears has, at its center, a single knotted rubber band. ("Putting something else in the middle is cheating," John says.) I'm not about to take it apart to find out.

For years the ball traveled from museum to gallery to museum on a flatbed truck. Last we heard, it was on display at Sloans & Kenyon, an auction house in Chevy Chase, Maryland. By the time you read this, it may be rolling around someone's living room.

As of winter 2006–2007, John was working on the world's largest bicycle inner-tube ball. "Not sure how much it weighs, but two full-grown men can't pick it up off the ground," he says. Go John!

BUCKS STOP HERE

If you want to save bucks: (1) don't hunt deer and (2) move to Delaware, where "How low can you go?" is the joyful song of home owners who enjoy paying super-low property taxes. No wonder they smile a lot. They have more coins for beer, new pickups, and the Dover Downs slots. Some other First State perks include no sales tax on goods, food, or entertainment. For seniors, Social Security and railroad-retirement benefits and up to $12,500 of investment and qualified pension income are exempt from income tax. Stove Top, I'm staying!

Delaware shines on pinstripers, too. Oh yeah—bright as the July sun on Rehoboth beachgoers. The business-friendly tax laws and efficient civil court system have put the state on the map. Little wonder that Delaware is a national center for corporations, banks, and credit card companies. Raising the UV index, the state's bankruptcy courts—once open forums—are a-changin'.

Take, for example, the case of the Werner Company. In June 2006 the ladder-making (as opposed to ladder–climbing) company filed for Chapter 11 reorganization in Delaware. The judge (Kevin J. Carey) agreed to seal documents about bonuses to Werner executives, deciding with company lawyers who argued that the disclosures might "harm morale" and contribute to "an unhealthy work environment." Puh-leeeze.

As quoted in the *New York Times,* law professor and author Lynn M. LoPucki said, "The big picture here is compensation of public-company executives during a bankruptcy case being kept secret, which if you believe in open courts, is not a good thing."

A Boy Named Judy
Wilmington

William Julius "Judy" Johnson is known as Delaware's folk hero of the (baseball) diamond. Johnson moved to Wilmington in 1905 from his Snow Hill, Maryland, birthplace at the age of five. Early on, the kid could hit a ball, and he would hang out with his father's local team.

Johnson debuted professionally with the Negro League in 1922 and was a top third baseman in the 1920s and 1930s. A natural talent, he was known for his contact hitting and maintaining a .300 or better batting average. Connie Mack is said to have told him, "If you were a white boy, you could name your own price." Don't surprise me none.

In 1954 Johnson became the first black assistant coach for a major-league team. As a major-league scout, he signed Bill Bruton to the Boston Braves; Bruton later became Johnson's son-in-law.

Judy Johnson was inducted into the National Baseball Hall of Fame in 1975. He died fourteen years later in Wilmington, where Johnson Field at Frawley Stadium bears his name. Oh, and in case you're wondering how he got the nickname Judy, my baseball sources say it came about because Johnson looked like Judy Gans, a Chicago American Giants player.

Butterflies Are Free
Wilmington

If you're into watching elusive, beautiful creatures, get out your field glasses and enjoy Delaware's butterflies—70 to 120 species, depending on who's counting. Though they're most prevalent spring through fall, some species hang around until December, weather permitting. Late August and September are best for viewing migrating monarchs. Lums Pond State Park, not far from the C & D Canal, near Bear, is primo. Who sez? Lepidopterists. They're entomologists (bug specialists) who further specialize in butterflies and moths.

If you can't get to the park, check out the butterfly garden adjacent to the Delaware Museum of Natural History patio in Wilmington (4840 Kennett Pike; 302–658–9111; www.delmnh.org). The butterflies l-o-v-e the colorful ageratum, butterfly weed, and asters.

While many disdain moths as occupying an inferior rung on the evolutionary ladder, many lepidopterists say moths belong to the same insect group as butterflies and should be included. Others distinguish between true butterflies and skippers, which are smaller than "true" butterflies and have angular wings and proportionately larger bodies. Hicky-picky. If they fly and have colorful wings, let's not allow semantics to get in the way.

A Du Pont by Any Other Name
Wilmington

There are nearly as many spellings for the Du Pont family as there are relatives, currently about 2,000 aboveground in the United States. Can you imagine the clan sitting down together at Christmas dinner? Maybe at Delaware Stadium.

Wealth and privilege may go hand in hand, but bucks don't buy spelling aptitude. In her book, *Henry F. du Pont and Winterthur: A Daughter's Portrait,* Ruth Lord talks about her father's spelling difficulties. She notes that, though highly musical, he had a tin ear when it came to words and once signed a letter to her sister *dady*.

Next time you're writing a term paper, bear in mind these nuances:

The food's good, but you have to dress for dinner.

- du Pont—a family member; space between *du* and *Pont*

- Du Pont—the whole damn family; space between *Du* and *Pont*

- DuPont—the chemical company; no spaces!

The name is said to have originated from the Old French *pont,* from the Latin *pons* for bridge. Hmm . . . bridge over Delaware Bay? Bridge over world-changing and earth-polluting chemicals?

Today the family still owns a lion's share of the company. *Roarrrr.*

BETTER THINGS FOR BETTER LIVING

DuPont is the world's largest chemical company, right? Wrong. They're No. 2, behind Dow. Don't whip out your handkerchief quite yet. With revenue of $28.5 billion in 2005, they must be doing something(s) right. In case you've forgotten, here's a sampling of familiar DuPont products. I'd bet my advance on this book (all 50 cents) that most, if not all, American homes have one or more of these:

Corian: Acrylic-based hard surface used in kitchens, baths, and furniture.

Glypure: High-purity glycolic acid used in cosmetics and dermatology.

Kevlar: Stronger-than-steel, heat-resistant fiber for fiber optics; asbestos substitute.

Lucite: Petrochemical plastic for a variety of defense, household, and decorative products.

Mylar: Strong polyester film descended from Dacron and cellophane.

Neoprene: Synthetic rubber; think fan belts, gaskets, hoses, waders, mouse pads.

Nylon: Tough, elastic synthetic polyamide commonly used for toothbrushes, stockings, fabrics, and ropes.

Teflon: Nonstick coating for cookware wiper blades, heavy-duty nail polish. Also many less interesting industrial uses.

Tyvek: Weather-resistant building wrap and medical packaging; also used as protective apparel.

Early Feminist Favored First State
Wilmington

One of the country's earliest feminist writers lived and worked for many years in Wilmington—decades before *feminist* had entered the popular lexicon. The biracial daughter of a seamstress and a sailor, Alice Ruth Moore began her life in New Orleans in 1875, but she spent her most productive years in the First State.

After graduating from Straight College in New Orleans, Alice taught in Harlem. Between quatrains and couplets she married noted poet Paul Laurence Dunbar. They moved to Washington, D.C., where, as Alice Dunbar, she published stories and poems flavored with the Creole dialect of her youth. She also split with Paul, then moved to Wilmington. Maybe it was for the pizza and museums. My sources were unsure.

Alice landed a teaching position at Wilmington's prestigious Howard High School, which played a pivotal role in educating blacks from 1867 on. (Today the school is a showcase for academics, athletics, and the arts.) During the summers she taught at the State College for Colored Students (now Delaware State University). Between teaching, chairing Howard's English department, and establishing its highly touted literary curriculum, Alice married a second time, but not for long.

Going for a hat trick, she married Robert J. Nelson, becoming Alice Dunbar-Nelson, and continued to publish essays, poetry, and newspaper articles. From 1920 to 1922 she coedited and published the Wilmington *Advocate* newspaper. An activist in the suffrage movement, she also worked tirelessly for passage of the Dyer Anti-Lynching Bill.

In 1932 she did the good-wife thing and followed Mr. Nelson to Philadelphia, where he had an appointment to the state boxing commission. Alice Dunbar-Nelson died in the City of Brotherly Love three years later, but her heart—and the rest of her, it turns out—belonged to Delaware. Following her wishes, she was cremated in Wilmington and her ashes were scattered over the Delaware River.

Getting High
Wilmington

What's Ebright Azimuth mean to you? An old school friend? A skin ailment requiring medical attention stat? A new element on the Periodic Table? Three strikes and you're out. Smack in the middle of Ebright Road, near the Delaware-Pennsylvania border, is the state's highest point. At 447.85 feet—or 448 or 451, depending on who's measuring—this is Delaware's Everest, according to the Delaware Geological Survey. Only Florida has a lower high point.

If you have nothing better to do and you're in the Wilmington area, why not trek to the top of Ebright Azimuth? From downtown Wilmington, take I–95 North to US 202/Concord Pike North. Go right at Naamans Road. Left at Ebright Road to Ramblewood Drive.

Before leaving home, remember to take medication for altitude sickness, put on your parka, and pack plenty of tissues for nosebleeds at the summit.

Gunpowder and Roses
Wilmington

Show of hands, please. What was the Du Pont family's first business? Chemical peels? Nope. Neoprene pizza? Uh-uh. Kevlar condoms? Sorry. Are you ready? Gunpowder.

In 1802 E. I. du Pont bought the Henry Clay Mill, formerly a cotton-spinning mill, and a 230-acre parcel on the Brandywine River. Ole E. I. (his friends called to him, "E. I., E. I., O . . . ") imported saltpeter from India and sulfur from Sicily (in later years from Mexico and Louisiana). For charcoal the workers burned willow branches that grew along the creek.

For 120 years the family manufactured black gunpowder in a mill with 5-foot-thick walls near the river, chosen because explosions would cause the least damage. Good move on someone's part—but not quite good enough. Despite their best efforts, there were 288 explosions and 258 fatalities.

Today you can visit the on-site Hagley Museum and Library and the family home and gardens, Eleutherian Mills, located at 298 Buck Road East, near the intersection of Routes 100 and 141. For more information call (302) 658–2400 or visit www.hagely.lib.de.us.

If the Shue Fits

Wilmington

Award-winning actress Elizabeth Shue was born October 6, 1963, in Wilmington, into a well-heeled family. Circumstances forced her to cross the Delaware Memorial Bridge into the Garden State, and she spent most of her youth in New Jersey. A good student, she excelled as a gymnast at Columbia High School in Maplewood. (Curious non-Delaware factoid: I went there, too. There the similarities end. I was never a good student, gymnast, actress, or blonde. And I'm old enough to be her mother.)

Shue shoved off for Wellesley College to study government. Between term papers she did TV commercials for Burger King and Hellmann's mayo, among others. She transferred to Harvard, studied poli-sci, and had aspirations to be a lawyer. But the tug of acting pulled her far from academia.

As a Harvard dropout, her career took off. Remember 1984's *The Karate Kid*? Playing Ralph Macchio's girlfriend was her breakthrough role. The well-respected actress has dozens of screen credits, most notably *Soapdish, Deconstructing Harry,* and *Leaving Las Vegas,* for

which she received several prestigious awards and an Academy Award nomination. (She should've been a shue-in!)

Fifteen years after leaving Harvard Square, she returned and got her degree in 2000. Today Shue balances her career with wifedom and motherhood.

Mmm, mmm Good
Wilmington

I don't know about you, but I'm content to slurp soup from any ole bowl—china or Chinet—and when I'm in a hurry, straight from the pot (please don't tell my mother). Many would never stoop to such soup abuse. Between stockpot and bowl, those to-the-manor-born ladled their chicken noodle into grand interim vessels before transferring the steaming liquid to matching covered dishes with two handles (écuelle, if you want to impress someone), which they would pick up and sip from. Why dirty a perfectly good spoon?

Everybody grab a spoon and dig in.

To get a taste of how the other half lived, feast your eyes on the Campbell Collection of Soup Tureens—also bowls, plates, spoons, and ladles—in the Dorrance Gallery at the Winterthur Museum (Route 52, 6 miles northwest of Wilmington; 800–448–3883; www.winterthur.org).

A showcase for more than one hundred beautifully crafted, sometimes whimsical tureens in porcelain, earthenware, and sculpted metals, the collection was started by John Dorrance, a Campbell Soup Company executive. After he died, the Campbell Museum donated the collection to Winterthur. Many of the pieces belonged to European royalty and nobility. For sure, nobody in my neighborhood has anything like it.

The tureen in the photo was made by the Chelsea Porcelain Factory, circa 1763. It was commissioned by King George III (aka Mad King George) and his wife, Queen Charlotte, for her brother, Duke Adolphus Frederick of Mecklenburg-Strelitz. Between then and 1966, when the Campbell Museum purchased it, the British Queen Mum was among the owners of the tureen, once part of a 132-piece service.

The animal and vegetable worlds are well represented elsewhere. On one tureen, rabbits chew on leaves as snails look on. Another is shaped like a boar's head—imagine it as the centerpiece of a formally set table, steam pouring from the boar's nostrils like saltwater from a neti pot. Others sport a chicken, rooster, swan, cabbage, and cauliflower. One, circa 1740, features eighteen scenes hand-painted on a gold background. (You wouldn't want to put that in the dishwasher.)

A visit to the Campbell Collection entertains and enlightens, acquainting those of us from society's lower crust with upper-crust eighteenth- and nineteenth-century dining practices. Then we can relax and go home to our chipped bowls.

A Roundabout Labor of Love
Wilmington

Henry F. du Pont was one sporty guy. He had lots of moola, a passion for Americana, and an eye for proportion and detail. He also loved his family. And he loved surprises. Sounds like a catch to me!

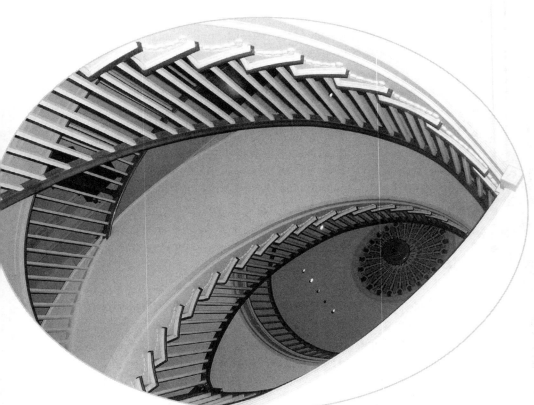

Do not climb these after two martinis.

While traveling around the world with his wife, Ruth Wales, and teenage daughters, Ruth Ellen and Pauline Louise, he arranged for workers to remove the marble and bronze staircase that stood in the entryway at Winterthur, the family cabin, and replace it with another. Piece of cake. The new one, freestanding and spiral in shape, was from an abandoned early nineteenth-century North Carolina house. When du Pont purchased it in 1935, it had to be taken apart and shipped—pre-FedEx—to Wilmington. Lesser mortals would have said *fuhgeddaboutit*. Not him. A stickler for detail, H. F. soldiered on. He was certain the work would proceed according to plan. His singular mission was to surprise his family on their return in May 1936. Nothing less would do.

That may have been his first mistake. Anyone who's taken hammer to nail knows there is always a hitch with remodeling projects, and this was no exception. In this case, the staircase didn't quite fit. Ouch! But H. F. had the resources and the determination. Some say the ovoid Montmorenci staircase was completed and installed less than a day before the family came home to Winterthur. That may be an exaggeration, but who cares? It's a great story—and it demonstrates the depth of his familial devotion. Nobody ever built me a staircase (though I got a bookshelf once).

The focal point for the bridal receptions of Pauline Louise and Ruth Ellen, the staircase is drop-dead gorgeous and appears to defy gravity. Decorated with evergreen roping and poinsettias, it is especially beautiful over the Christmas holidays at Winterthur (Route 52, 6 miles northwest of Wilmington; 800–448–3883; www.winterthur.org).

Staging Area
Wilmington

So what's the big deal about a theater in a city of 73,000? Well, for one thing, Wilmington's stately DuPont Theatre, "the oldest continually operating legitimate theater in the nation," is in the luxurious Hotel DuPont, where Charles Lindbergh, Ingrid Bergman, Eleanor Roosevelt, JFK, and other notables have bedded down (but not together).

The theater, underwritten by three DuPont executives (among them, Pierre S. du Pont), opened to great fanfare on October 15, 1913. Call me a name-dropper, but among those who've performed here are Helen Hayes, Orson Welles, Ethel Merman, Robert Redford, Julie Andrews, Tommy Tune, and Joel Grey. The theater-in-a-hotel concept puts ice-making machines and honor bars in proper perspective, don't you think? Book a room, don your duds, have a divine meal in the elegant Green Room, and slip into your orchestra seat. No traffic woes, no parking problems, no hassles.

My big break and I'm playing to an empty house.

Now here's something curious. When the theater is dark, it's available for private functions. Imagine holding your corporate retreat, bar mitzvah, or wedding in the 1,252-seat space. You could banish unpopular family members or difficult staff to the balcony. Park your kids or your in-laws in the orchestra pit. The possibilities are endless. Those reserving the theater—for their next cousins club or bridge tournament—have the use of the production staff, house manager, stage/lighting/sound crew, dressing rooms (including two designated for "stars"), and two washers and dryers.

The DuPont Theatre is located at Tenth and Market Streets. Call (800) 338–0881 or visit www.playhousetheatre.com for more information.

THE MANEUVERER

Dr. Henry J. Heimlich, the inventor of the maneuver that, since 1974, has saved countless victims from choking to death, was born in Wilmington on February 3, 1920. While the maneuver that made him famous has grown in disfavor, Heimlich is not losing any sleep. In the medical community he is better known for developing a valve used to treat patients with massive chest wounds and an esophageal replacement. But since the Heimlich Institute is in Cincinnati, where he resides, I guess I'll have to end here.

Sub Wars
Wilmington

I couldn't get my hands on the latest statistics, but I'm willing to bet a jar of hot peppers that every Wilmington resident over the age of two months consumes, on average, one hundred times his/her body weight per annum in subs, aka hoagies or grinders. A sandwich by any other name tastes as scrumptious and must meet this criterion: When you're eating it, oil should drip down your arm.

Writer finds inspiration in Italian cold cut sub.

A warning to out-of-staters: Don't get caught in the crossfire of a sub war. It isn't pretty. Think I'm kidding? Couples have split and family members have stopped speaking to each other over who makes the best sub, and why. Escalations occur over whose bread is tastiest, freshest, and has the best texture; who piles on the most cold cuts; which cheesesteak has the tenderest beef; and the merits of traditional processed cheese versus provolone. Don't say I didn't give you a heads-up.

If you've just landed from Uranus and don't know what a sub is, try at least one of these all-inclusive delicious meals on a roll. It would be a sin not to. Another sin is to ask for mayo on your sub. Trust me, you don't need mayo. There is enough oil on a sub to heat every home in Delaware for a fortnight. Delawareans are pretty forgiving, but the mayo faux pas is a no-no. Up the road in Philly—the Lourdes of subs—you would be shot for the travesty.

Try any or all of these and report back:

Grotto Pizza (1819 Pennsylvania Avenue; 302–777–3278; www.grottopizza.com). Founded in 1960, Grotto is best known for its pizza—quite simply, the best on the planet Earth. If you're not in a pizza mood, try one of the dozen varieties of subs. (I don't count the Sizzlin' Hot Dog. A hot dog is a hot dog, *capiche*?) The meatball is my fave. You're never far from a Grotto, *grazie a Dio,* with sixteen locations throughout the state.

Capriotti's (510 North Union Street; 302–571–8929; www.capriottis .com). Capriotti's opened in this Union Street brick row house in 1976, and it's still going strong. Since then Cap's has added thirteen eateries in Delaware while spreading the yum-yum in other states near and far. Build a better sandwich, and the world will beat a path to your counter. Cap's logo is a turkey. Why? Because it invented the Bobbie sub— turkey, cranberry sauce, stuffing, and mayo—a legendary best seller. Don't make a face! It's delish. I may serve it Thanksgiving instead of spending two months in the kitchen and another two cleaning up. Some of us try really hard not to salivate on the counter while awaiting a large (20-inch) cheesesteak with fried onions.

Casapulla's (514 Casapulla Avenue; 302–994–5934). So many choices, so little room. When indecision paralyzes me, I get a small cheesesteak and a small Italian cold cut. Call me an equal-opportunity eater—and life is too short to be conflicted. I don't know what they do to the bread, but it has a great texture and a slightly crunchy crust. True love comes in many guises, and without a doubt, this is one of them. Casapulla's has six locations—one hopes more are on the way.

Happy eating!

Wooden-Nyckel Watchdogs
Wilmington

The *Kalmar Nyckel* is the state's most visible goodwill ambassador, an authentic replication of the vessel that brought the area's first settlers to present-day Wilmington in 1638. But who let those dogs on the Wilmington-based tall ship? At first glance the wooden canines look like they're sleeping, but closer inspection reveals that they are, indeed, half-awake. Each animal (one port, one starboard) has its waterside eye open. Peg Tigue of the Kalmar Nyckel Foundation explains that "they're keeping an eye on the ocean for changes in the weather." These carvings of "weather dogs," done by seven volunteers, are historically accurate and were thought to ward off evil spirits. Aiding the dogs, a lion stands sentry on the bow.

The *Kalmar Nyckel* is yar (fit and beautiful)—139 feet long and 64 feet tall, with ten cannons, two swivel guns, and fifty hand-carved figures. The all-volunteer crew that keeps her shipshape occupies twenty-eight racks (bunks), but only when they're not hoisting or lowering canvas, performing chores, or on watch. The *Kalmar*'s top speed under full sail is 12 knots. Hey, it's the journey that counts. What's the hurry?

The Royal Swedish Navy purchased the original Dutch-built ship in 1628, naming it after the city of Kalmar. The *Kalmar Nyckel* left in December 1637 with a crew of twenty-four Swedes, Finns, Germans, and Dutch, and hit bad weather in the North Sea. (Big surprise. Why didn't they wait until spring?) They holed up in Holland for repairs, downed a few Amstels, and then set sail again, arriving in present-day Wilmington where they established the Colony of New Sweden in March 1638.

For more information, including a schedule of events, call (302) 429–7447 or visit www.kalmar nyckel.org.

Cover for me while I take a nap.

Ye Olde Homesteade
Wilmington

Descended from Burgundian noblemen, Pierre Samuel du Pont de Nemours (can you say it fast five times?) was born in 1739. The son of a watchmaker, he was a Parisian playwright but no threat to Neil Simon. Wisely, he turned his attention elsewhere and became a successful businessman and politician. Always well connected, he was rewarded with a coat of arms for his role in negotiating the Treaty of Paris in 1783. When he'd had it with Parisian politics, he crossed the pond—some say just ahead of his creditors—with his wife, Nicole Charlotte Marie Louise le Dée de Rencourt (Nicki, for short?); sons Victor Marie and Eleuthere Irenee (founder of the future E. I. du Pont de Nemours and Company); and millions of francs.

No fool, Pierre started out in New York, where he had good connections like then vice president Thomas Jefferson. (Mom and Dad were right: It's not what you know, but who you know.) The family settled outside Wilmington in Delaware's Brandywine River Valley. Homesick for baguettes and chocolate mousse, Pierre went to Paris for a spell, returning to Wilmington before his death. His entrepreneurial son E. I., he of the Midas touch, took the ball and ran with it, laying the groundwork for the family's chemical empire. E. I. also invested heavily in banks and businesses, and the family's wealth skyrocketed.

Eight generations after Pierre landed in the New World, the Du Ponts remain among America's wealthiest families. Their passion for horticulture and American decorative arts is unprecedented and on view at several museums throughout the Wilmington area, but especially at Winterthur (pronounced *WIN-tur-toor*), the best-known property.

E. I.'s daughter, Evelina Gabrielle, and her husband, James Bider-mann, can take credit for that purchase. When they departed this world, the original three-story Greek Revival house, built in 1839, fell fortuitously into the hands of their grand-nephew, Henry F. du Pont. We can all thank Henry for putting ye olde homesteade on the map. He had a major thing for American furniture and fine and decorative arts. In 1951, with his personal collection surpassing in breadth and depth those of most museums, the family created a nonprofit and opened Winterthur (Route 52, 6 miles northwest of Wilmington; 800–448–3883; www.winterthur.org) to the public.

If you haven't been, we're talking about 175 period rooms and three galleries in two buildings. Mind-blowing, heart-stopping, exquisite. And the gardens? Magnificent, especially in spring when the azaleas bloom. On second thought, the roses are stupendous, too.

Today the family still owns a lion's share of the company. *Roarrrr.*

CENTRAL DELAWARE

NEW JERSEY

Smyrna

Bombay Hook

KENT COUNTY

Dover

Little Creek

Port Mahon

Dover Air Force Base

DUPONT HIGHWAY

MARYDEL

MARYLAND

Felton

Harrington

MISPILLION RIVER

DELAWARE BAY

0   10 Miles

0   10 KM

CENTRAL DELAWARE

Kent County

Keeping things simple is easy in a state with only three counties. Technically, Central Delaware is Kent County, lying between New Castle to the north and Sussex to the south. Central Delaware/Kent County is a little of this and a little of that, as my grandmother used to say. In Dover, the state capital, rabble-rousers met in secret to plot revolution against Great Britain, and Delaware delegates were the first to ratify the U.S. Constitution (hence the nickname "First State"). Today history bumps noses with high-tech on a daily basis.

Don't be surprised to see bonneted Amish women shopping at an open-air market next to suits and briefcases, or buggies clopping alongside Beemers. Military planes (some larger than the county itself) roar in and out of Dover AFB regularly. On North Dupont Highway, NASCAR and Dover Downs slot machines draw their share of fans. To the east, wildlife areas and bay beaches beckon those in search of natural entertainment. Field glasses and guidebooks in hand, birders flock spring and fall to Bombay Hook in Smyrna to view migrating shorebirds and waterfowl. All in all, Central Delaware has its share of odd birds.

WHAT STREET ARE WE ON?

I've driven in all but seven of the United States. I would say, as respectfully as I can, that Delaware's signage is among the most challenging. Here are a few examples:

The mailing address for the Little Creek Inn in Dover is 2623 North Little Creek Road. However, the road on which the property sits, between U.S. Highway 13 and Route 9, is alternately signed Route 8, Division Street, North Little Creek Road, King's Highway, and Forest Avenue.

Once, in New Castle, I drove for days looking for a motel on US 13. Euphoric when I passed a sign declaring it to be "3 miles ahead on the right," I was surprised ten minutes and 6 miles later to see WELCOME TO WILMINGTON. I pulled into the lot of a bowling alley and asked a patron for directions. He said he was traveling in that direction and led me to the property. That's Delaware.

The ganglion of north–south highways and roads around Dover is like an anatomy exam. I suggest implementing color-coded stripes or guardrails. It may be that highway planners are testing drivers' patience and coping skills for a psychological study. What can I say? Take a chill pill, use GPS, and travel during daylight hours whenever possible.

CENTRAL DELAWARE

No Exit

Dover

When it came to handing out exits on I–95 in Delaware, it appears that someone was asleep at the drawing board, or sign board. Consider this: There are exit 1 and exits 3 through 11, but no 2. Helloooo . . . Has anyone seen exit 2? Suppose your friends invited you to a party at their new house and told you to get off the interstate at exit 2. What would you do, especially if your car lacked GPS and you left the cell phone charging on the kitchen counter? You might spend the rest of your life searching in vain—and without benefit of beverage or cold meatballs.

According to my friend Jack (a Delaware historian who knows *jack*!), here is the backstory. When President Kennedy cut the ribbon for the Delaware Turnpike (I–95) on November 14, 1963, the road was an extension of the Northeast Expressway in Maryland. In logical fashion, the exits followed sequentially from Maryland through Delaware. A week after the ribbon-cutting, the president was assassinated, and the road was designated the John F. Kennedy Memorial Highway. A decade later the present numbering system came into play. (Maybe it was a slow day at the state highway administration.)

Exit 2, I am told, was slated to be the Pike Creek Freeway (US 301). So far, so good. One small problem, though—the road was never built. So the next time you're traversing I–95 in Delaware and searching for a restaurant, point of interest, or long-lost relative, do yourself a favor and get off at exit 1 or 3.

No White Cliffs in Sight
Dover

Here's a guest-stumper for your next party: What's the capital of Delaware? If you live in one of the other forty-nine states, I wouldn't be surprised if your otherwise highly educated and sophisticated guests don't have a clue. *Uh, Wilmington? Rehoboth? Philadelphia?* With a population hovering around 34,000, it's hardly Gotham. And there's not a white cliff in sight of this Dover, the third point of a triangle joining Philadelphia and Washington, D.C. But it's made its mark. You don't think so? Consider these milestones in the city's colorful history.

William (Billy to insiders) Penn founded Dover in 1683 on a slow day at the track. In 1777 the state capital was moved from New Castle to Dover; ten years later, Delaware was the first of the original thirteen colonies to ratify the Constitution—on December 7, 1787, if you care. In 1881, after fires devastated Dover, the town fathers established a water system. Good move. Doverites turned on electric lights for the first time in the early 1900s. Then not much happened for a while. (Hey, I have only 300 words!)

My wife thinks I'm bowling.

CENTRAL DELAWARE

The town grew after World War I and the opening in 1924 of the Dupont Highway, the state's blacktop spine. International Laytex Corporation set up shop in 1937—the first big business not connected with chickens, corn, or wheat. You'll rest easier knowing that the company split into Playtex Apparel, Inc. (Cross Your Heart bras and other lingerie) and Playtex Products, Inc. (Binky pacifiers and Diaper Genie, skin-care and grooming aids). After World War II Dover Air Force Base settled on the outskirts of town and things took off. (Ouch!)

Dover is chockablock with history and interesting sights, natural and man-made. Go! It's a great place to visit. Cross my Playtex-warmed heart. For information call the Kent County Tourism office at (800) 233–KENT or check out www.visitdover.com.

Fleas Come

Dover

Searching for cowboy boots? Recycled toilets? Cookware? Donuts? Quilts? Belts? Bug repellent? Baskets? Aluminum foil? Corn on the cob? Clothing that may have fallen off the back of a truck? For all this and more, there's Spence's Bazaar (550 South New Street; 302–734–3441). It's where you'll find an unusual gift for that person who has (almost) everything. For example, on my last visit, my romantic companion wowed me with a canister of Fart Spray. Some women get jewelry, I get . . . never mind. And it wasn't even my birthday! Would I kid you? Every home should have some. Works like a charm when guests overstay their welcome.

Spence's auctions are something else—some of the merchandise would be lucky to find a loving dumpster. Arriving hungry is a must. Lots of folks tote coolers so they can both feed their faces on-site (there are plenty of picnic tables) and take goodies home for later. I'm talking

Just the right size for my inheritance.

sausages, Lebanon bologna, prepared foods (don't miss the pork BBQ), and fresh produce, cheeses, and baked goods, most from the local Amish community. The line for ice-cream sundaes is long for good reason. Be still my heart.

At Spence's the goods and eats are reasonably priced. Better yet, the people-watching is free—and priceless.

BAMBI, GO HOME!

Oh deer! In spring 2006 state wildlife officials hired USDA marksmen to aid hunters who typically (and voluntarily) bring in their harvest. Do I detect the influence of ole S. S. (Sure Shot) Cheney here? The state called in the pros to help with a study on deer reproductive habits. (I sure hope this doesn't translate to the human sector.) Studying deer's mating habits—like whether they say yes on the first date or smoke a cigarette afterward—will help the state to better manage the deer population. As with most things, there's more to this than meets the gun barrel, er, eye.

According to Joe Rogerson, a game mammal biologist for the state, when local hunters brought in "only 152 female deers, after four state-run checks in January 2006, well short of the 600 goal, we went to Plan B and called in USDA wildlife services." After surveying Delaware's three counties, the state concluded that deer in high-density areas have lower reproductive rates, and vice versa. Well-nourished fawns reach maturity and breed, Rogerson says, but many are overstressed in high-density areas. (Aren't we all?) As a result, relatively few reach maturity. Makes sense to me.

The public perception that deer breed like rabbits is wrong-o. Rogerson says that deer usually carry two fetuses, but not all survive owing to predators, poor nutrition, the high divorce rate, and in-law problems—OK, I threw in the last two to see if you were paying attention.

We wish the state happy hunting and good luck with the study. If USDA marksmen fall short of their quota, one wonders if the state will call in the Delaware National Guard. Deer me!

The Flight Stuff

Dover

The C-5 Galaxy, 247 feet long and with a fuel capacity of 51,000 gallons, can hold 7 helicopters, 6 commercial-size buses, or 25,844,746 ping pong balls. Who am I to argue? And who in the world would have the time or patience to load them? Several times a week Mike Leister, director of the Air Mobility Command (AMC) museum at Dover AFB, pushes away from his desk to lead tours through the hangar (historic planes, nose art, flight simulator, and incredible stories). For me the pièce de résistance of the tour is parked on the flight line. Mike gestures to a C-5, a cargo plane so gargantuan it looks like it couldn't possibly leave the ground. Thanks to Mike's chatty delivery, the history slides down as easily as ice cream. We're lucky because not only is the C-5 not always there, when it is, it's rarely open to the public.

I listen intently. Can't believe I had resisted coming. Thought I'd be bored. Ha! I learn that when the C-5's front and rear cargo areas are open (ideally, only on the ground at a full stop) crews can load and off-load simultaneously. Bearing the weight of a full load are *28* wheels. Cheap insurance when that cargo is a 74-ton mobile scissors bridge. Each of the 4 TF39 turbofan engines weighs close to 8,000 pounds— and each has 43,000 pounds of thrust. I don't know squat about thrust. And numbers are not my thing. But, I will tell you, these suckers are *huge*. Can you imagine performing an aerial refueling on a moving target this size?

Next Mike shows us the C-133—and it's pretty impressive—with its ability to hold three school buses on its own. Then he continues to regale his rapt audience with the story of a visiting aerial engineer who had flown the C-47 in WW II. The vet climbed a ladder, felt inside the fuselage and located shrapnel damage. Still there. Anytime you can, fly over here. The view is great. (Air Mobility Command Museum, south of Dover on Route 9 East, 1.2 miles off 113; 302–677–5938; www.amcmuseum.org. Open Tuesday through Friday, 9:00 A.M. to 4:00 P.M.).

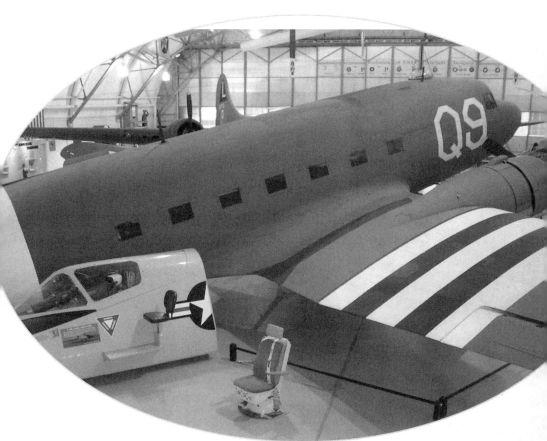

A World War II Vet enjoys retirement.

Hail, Caesar (Rodney)
Dover

Back in the 1990s the U.S. Treasury began issuing quarters for each state. Because Delaware was the first state to ratify the U.S. Constitution, the Delaware coin was the first one out of the U.S. Mint hopper. 'Twas one of those rare instances when the government does something that makes sense.

If you turn over a Delaware quarter, the reverse (I almost said *backside*) is an image of patriot Caesar Rodney on horseback. But you can't see Rodney's face—he turns away. Did we do something to offend him? Was it a show of disrespect on the part of the artist or some U.S. Mint*ee*? No. Cancer disfigured Rodney's face, and he was so self-conscious, it is said, that he sometimes covered it with a silk scarf. To this day there are statues, but no portraits, of Rodney. And leaving the story here would be to show Rodney the same disrespect afforded another Rodney (Dangerfield, that is).

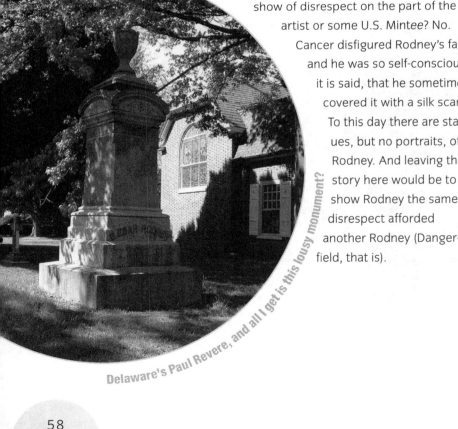

Delaware's Paul Revere, and all I get is this lousy monument?

CENTRAL DELAWARE

A great patriot, Caesar Rodney is often referred to as the Paul Revere of Delaware. He was a Renaissance guy. This delegate to the Continental Congress was also a soldier, a judge, and Speaker of the Assembly (and I understand he was nice to his mother). Debilitated by cancer and asthma, he rode the 80 miles from Dover to Philadelphia (either by horseback or carriage—it's still up for debate) in a heat wave and through thunderstorms, arriving at Independence Hall in the nick of time to cast the tie-breaking vote for independence. (*NOTE*: He arrived on July 2, not July 4, 1776, the date the document was approved. Just another curious factoid from the annals of American history.)

Fast forward to the selection process for the Delaware state quarter. Three designs were chosen from a field of more than 300 entries. Several committees did what committees do—slowly. They OK'd the concepts then turned them over to a citizens' poll. About three-quarters of those queried said Rodney should appear on the coin. The final design, you won't be surprised to learn, came from an art teacher at . . . Caesar Rodney High School in Dover.

If you want to pay your respects to Rodney, visit his monument at the Christ Episcopal Church Cemetery in Dover (501 South State at Water Street) or Wilmington's Rodney Square (Ninth and King Streets). If you want to hail Caesar more, drive two hours south to the U.S. Capitol's National Statuary Hall, where he represents Delaware in marble.

Which way is Philadelphia?

His Master's Voice
Dover

Many of us over a certain age played records on a Victrola. (Yes, way before audiotapes, CDs, and iPods, and no, I don't need help crossing the street.) Few icons are as recognizable from the early days of recorded music as the image of Nipper the dog, peering into the cylindrical speaker of a gramophone, and the immortal words "His Master's Voice."

In Dover's historic district is the Johnson Victrola Museum (Museum Square, 375 South New Street; 302–739–4266; www.history.delaware.gov/museums), honoring native son Eldridge Reeves Johnson, inventor of the Victrola version of the "talking machine" and owner of the Victor Talking Machine Co. Thank you, State of Delaware, for pulling together this remarkable collection of early talking and recording machines, recordings, and other music-related memorabilia. Nearly overshadowing Johnson here is Nipper—branding machines and records, and immortalized in paintings, drawings, sculptures, and souvenirs. Who was this dog? And what was his relationship to E. R. Johnson? I thought you'd never ask . . .

As is the case with many geniuses, Johnson was an inquisitive but poor student. According to his biography, his headmaster at the Dover Academy told him to learn a trade because he was "too dumb to go to college." (Bet you know where this is going.) So Johnson, who loved to tinker, apprenticed in Philadelphia and Camden, New Jersey, machine shops. In short order he proved his mettle and bought out his employer. Some dummy, eh? On hearing an early Berliner gramophone in 1896, Johnson said to himself, I can do better. And he did, dedicating the rest of his life to recording science.

Meanwhile, across the pond, British artist Francis Barraud painted a portrait of his dog, Nipper, who liked listening to the family phonograph while searching for the voice's origin. The artist painted the dog in this pose and showed it to Gramophone Co. Ltd. manager William Owen, who agreed to purchase the work on the condition that Barraud substitute a gramophone made by his partner, Emile Berliner. Barraud was a better painter than businessman. He made the change and received only 100 pounds (50 for the copyright, 50 for the painting).

If I keep still, maybe they won't notice me.

In 1900 Owen and Berliner registered the new trademark. Then along came entrepreneur E. R. Johnson, who set up shop with O&B, acquired the rights to the "His Master's Voice" trademark, and founded the Victor Talking Machine Company in 1901. RCA bought the Victor Company from bankers in 1929, and the rest, as they say, is history.

Oops, I almost forgot the pooch. Barraud's descendants have said that Nipper, who appears benign in art and ads, was so named because he nipped the backs of visitors' legs. And you thought it was because of his fondness for whiskey. Poor Nipper—his third cousin woofed that he died intestate. Today he'd come back from the grave and sue for back royalties.

If you're interested, the original Nipper painting hangs in London at EMI Music, which evolved from Berliner's Gramophone Co. And E. R. Johnson's headmaster continues to spin in his grave.

A Necessary Chair
Dover

When you're in Dover's historic 'hood, I urge you to stop at the Sewell C. Biggs Museum of American Art (the Biggs, for short) at 406 Federal Street (302–674–2111; www.biggsmuseum.org). If you bump into Ryan, the curator, say hello and mention my name. We have a little bet going. Not to worry—it's on the up and up.

Among the Biggs's stunning portraits and landscapes, furniture, silver, and other decorative arts spanning the mid-eighteenth century to the present day is the Necessary chair in Gallery One. Well, aren't all chairs necessary, especially when your feet hurt, or it's mealtime, or the big game is about to begin? Just how necessary was this chair? I'll let you decide. It's a twofer—a combination stately armchair and chamber (or night) chair all in one. Get it? You could be entertaining guests and relieving yourself at the same time. No need to interrupt a scintillating conversation or leave the room.

A step up from the iconic chamber pot—in most cases, a ceramic bowl-shaped vessel with a handle that was stored discretely under the bed, with or without a lid—the Necessary chair was a genteel alternative. This one, in late Chippendale style, was made in the Delaware Valley sometime between 1765 and 1790. Crafted of mahogany and Atlantic white cedar, it once belonged to Jacob and Mary Swab. (Lovely couple, the Swabs . . .) No colonial yuppie home was without a Necessary chair, more than one if they were *nouveau yup,* until the nineteenth century when WCs (water closets) were introduced into American homes.

The original dining room restroom.

If you wish to craft a Necessary chair for your own home, it's as easy as A-B-P. First, make a chair frame. Next, find a board for the seat and cut the *necessary* hole. Attach a deep ceramic or pewter bowl to the board. Make sure it fits snugly—very snugly. Add a deep apron to the chair frame to conceal the chamber pot. Finally, fashion an upholstered lift-off seat to cover the board. I'm surprised Home Depot doesn't sell kits.

TIMED OUT

The Biggs Museum of American Art opened its doors in 1998 due to the largesse of its benefactor. I don't know if he ever collected etchings, but his fine and decorative arts are a sight for sore eyes. Maybe you never heard of Sewell C. Biggs. That's OK—he probably never heard of you either.

Born in 1915 in Middletown (down the road a piece from Dover), Biggs graduated from the University of Delaware; went to law school for a spell; studied architecture at Harvard, Oxford, and Cambridge; and, in 1937, traveled around the world, fueling his lifelong interest in art conservation and historic preservation.

The guy had major smarts. And class. He also possessed a very healthy ego. Before donating his clock collection to the museum, he set each and every one to 11:05, the time of his birth. On January 16, 2003, his time ran out, but his clocks still read 11:05.

Stars in Her Eyes
Dover

Born during the Civil War, Annie Jump Cannon hardly fit the Scarlett O'Hara mold. Miss Annie set her sights much, much higher than on Rhett Butler and Ashley Wilkes types. This gal had stars in her eyes. Some might compare her to a supernova.

At an early age Annie turned her gaze toward the sky, an interest some say she inherited from her mother. A star pupil at her Dover high school, she enrolled at Wellesley College in 1880. Perhaps owing to the cold, damp New England weather, she contracted scarlet fever and lost her hearing. But infirmity did not keep her earthbound.

After graduating in 1884 Annie returned to Dover. Bored with the rural life, she wrote to her former professor in physics and astronomy, asking for work as an assistant, and got it. She bid adieu to Dover and returned to Wellesley, where she took grad courses in physics and astronomy, developed a passion for photography, and learned about spectroscopy (a way to measure and interpret the interplay of radiant energy with matter). Just your typical nineteenth-century southern belle. Not. Always reaching beyond her grasp, she signed up at Radcliffe in order to use Harvard's celestial observatory. She stayed at Harvard for most of the rest of her life.

From 1915 to 1924 alone, it's said, she catalogued more than 225,000 stars and distinguished herself as a "world expert." By the end of her life, Annie Jump Cannon had classified about 350,000 stars. Not bad for a small-town girl from Dover, Delaware—or anyone (male or female) from anywhere, for that matter. Her efforts led to the definitive work on star cataloguing, the Henry Draper Catalogue of Classification.

Perhaps her hearing loss allowed her to concentrate solely on her work, as some posit. No matter. In her prime she is said to have classified three new stars per minute—and that was in sparsely populated areas. She died at the age of seventy-six, having accrued a long list of awards and degrees. And the Cannon moon crater is named for her. Fiddly dee.

What's a New York Couple Doing in a Place Like This?
Dover

What are two die-hard New Yorkers doing in a bed-and-breakfast outside of Dover? This is not a trick question. The short answer: They own it.

Talk about going from the sublime to the ridiculous—or, in this case, chichi East Hampton, Long Island, to Dover, Dela*where?* In 1998 Bobby and Carol Thomas traded two homes and a successful restaurant, where Bobby was dishing up to a thousand meals *a day,* for a circa 1860 Italianate mansion a few miles from downtown Dover. "You're working too hard," Carol recalls telling her husband. "You retire and play golf; I'll run a little B&B."

Nowadays Bobby Thomas works harder than ever—and he's only too happy to tell you about it. "We're the gardeners, pool people, and maintenance workers. I help change the sheets when the maid doesn't show up." A member of the James Beard Society, he started in the hospitality business as a waiter, bartender, bouncer—"head bouncer"—and restaurant manager in New York City. Together the couple owned the Eastern Seafood Co. restaurant (first in East Hampton, then in the city). In between they had an inn in the Hudson Valley. Carol's exquisite taste and years as an interior designer are evident throughout the bed-and-breakfast.

Bobby is often in the kitchen before dawn, baking muffins for guests, who start the day with a full breakfast—fresh fruit, an omelet or other egg dish, bread and muffins, and plenty of piping hot java or tea—in the sunny yellow dining room with fresh-cut flowers on each table.

Sometimes he's preparing a meal for a group or re-creating Capt. Charlie's Chowder, the soup his grandfather created and sold from a pushcart on Lower Broadway.

"We looked in the Carolinas," Carol says. "We thought, been there, done that." When Bobby read an article about the Eastern Shore of Virginia, they decided to take a look. It rained for three days. "We liked it . . . but there were no people!" he says. Too tired to complete the drive back to Long Island, they overnighted in Dover. The next morning, they followed a sign to Little Creek. There, at 2623 North Little Creek Road, sat their house-to-be, the Little Creek Inn (302–730–1300; www.little creekinn.com) wearing a FOR SALE sign. These days a welcoming committee—yellow Labs Jake and Hank—greets arriving visitors.

Nobody ever makes breakfast for me.

SEX ON THE BEACH

(Warning: The following contains information that may be unsuitable for kids.)

Delaware is the bedroom for a mating ritual that has been going on for more than 350 *million* years—predating dinosaurs, birds, and Britney and Kevin ("FedEx"). Voyeurs convene on Delaware Bay beaches between Port Mahon and Broadkill every May during the full moon to watch horseshoe crabs (actually arachnids like spiders and scorpions) drag their sorry armored selves onto the sand to do what comes naturally. How do the crabs know when to get it on? Some scientists say the rising water temperature tells 'em (the crabs, not the voyeurs) it's time to splash on some aftershave or eau de toilette. (I'm just relaying info. In my wildest fantasy, I couldn't have made this up.)

R-Rated

The females dig holes in the sand, lay about 20,000 eggs—4,000 or so per drop. In a variation on Sadie Hawkins Day, the female, twice as large as the male, picks a partner and drags him over the eggs. He clamps his hooklike front legs onto her back and several other males cluster around, in case Choice #1 turns out to be a loser. The males deposit their sperm on the eggs, cover the eggs with sand and skedaddle back to the water. About two weeks later the crablets crawl to the water, feeding on worms and shellfish along the way. Those that survive will molt many times over a 10-year period before earning the privilege of having . . . sex on the beach.

Chain, Chain, Chain

Besides producing itty bitty horseshoe-crab babies, the species contributes to the food chain. Shorebirds bulk up on the crab eggs during their spring migration. Environmentalists and commercial

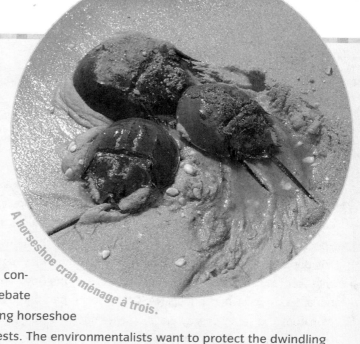

A horseshoe crab ménage à trois.

fishermen continue to debate over limiting horseshoe crab harvests. The environmentalists want to protect the dwindling number of shorebirds. The fishermen rely on crabs as bait (for eel and conch). And so it goes.

More than a Pretty Face

Biomedical studies of the crab's compound eyes have led to breakthroughs in treating diseases of the human eye. And the crab's copper-based blue blood, which has nothing at all to do with its lineage, has a clotting factor, lysate, that detects bacteria. Pharmaceutical companies use the lysate to determine the purity of injectable meds and implanted devices.

A Little R-e-s-p-e-c-t

The next time you see a beached horseshoe crab, show a little respect. It may not be as cute as a panda or a dolphin, but it won't harm you. The spiky tail is for mobility only. If you spot a horseshoe crab on its back, flip it over gently from the side of the shell.

A Be Humane to Horseshoe Crabs message.
Paid for by Friends of H.S. Crabs, Inc.

Thunder Road
Dover

Begun in 1948 NASCAR (National Association for Stock Car Auto Racing) is a fine madness—a sport that's been growing in popularity with each passing pileup, I mean, year. This is big business, boys and girls. Speedways are popping up like mushrooms all over the landscape. If you don't have a track within 50 miles of your driveway, you probably will—sooner rather than later. Fans converge on the Dover International Speedway when it hosts NASCAR races as part of the Nextel (Winston) Cup series every June and September. It's a big deal in Delaware. Bigger even than the senior prom. Or your first wedding.

NASCAR drivers (and fans) are hooked on speed.

From late April through October, those with the desire and the shekels can take a turn behind the wheel or ride with an experienced driver around the same track as the experts. Before you get too excited, you must be sixteen to ride along, eighteen to drive. A clean driving record helps. The program is known as the Monster Racing Experience (800–468–6946, ext. 110; www.monsterracing.com). Most first-timers reach a speed of 90 mph on the straightaway, I'm told. Trying to take the corners at 90 is not a good idea, however.

I haven't had the pleasure yet, but I'm wait-listed. Sound like fun? Reserve a time slot (8:00 A.M. or 12:30 P.M.) from six months to a year in advance. The cost includes classroom time and the use of a racing suit, helmet, and other safety equipment. Bandages are extra. Reservations are required for all but the basic Ride the Monster (four laps with an instructor). Treat someone you love (or hate) to Drive the Monster (twenty laps). If you want to sign up for thirty laps or more, trust me, they'll be happy to accommodate you. A Monster Racing gift certificate sure beats socks or fruitcake at Christmas.

BORDER PATROL

Straddling the border between Maryland and Delaware, a few miles west of Dover, is the town of Marydel. If you want someone to snap your picture with one leg in each state, head for 39.112 N latitude, 75.744 W longitude on Route 8.

Blast from the Past

Felton

About 10 miles south of Dover lives a dinosaur who awakens only on weekends. The last (outdoor) picture show in Delaware is the Diamond State Drive-In (U.S. Highway 13 South and Plymouth Road; 302–284–8307; www.dsdit.com), one of only around 800 drive-ins in the entire country. The first, for you trivia buffs, opened in 1933 across the river in Camden, New Jersey. Drive-ins peaked in the 1950s, when they numbered about 3,775.

Albert and Mildred Steele opened the Diamond State in 1949. Everything old is new again. Today in the snack house you can still buy mosquito-repellant coils along with your burger and nachos. In its early days a small performance stage sat under the screen, about 10 feet off the ground. By the early 1980s you could catch adult-only films at the Diamond State. Maybe that had something to do with why it closed in 1985. Nobody's saying. As you might imagine, the weeds grew tall and the site fell into disrepair.

A decade later it reopened, all spruced up and with a new agenda— first-run family fare instead of heavy breathing and bodice ripping. I wonder if teenagers still go to drive-ins to "make out." *How quaint.*

Waiting for the action to begin.

72

Crazy Over Horses
Harrington

Visit Chick's 30,000-square-foot showroom and warehouse on US 13, and you'll be hard-pressed to imagine that Frank Chick, a third-generation horseman, started the business in 1974 from the trunk of his car. When he outgrew the trunk, he moved the operation into his mother's Oxford, Pennsylvania, garage for a while.

In 1978 Chick gave mom back her garage and moved to Harrington, where he sold halters, harnesses, and the like to harness racers—usually out of box vans, according to his wife, Linda. Necessity pushed him to rent a warehouse, using part of it as a retail operation. Then customers with riding horses started coming in. Business picked up, and again Chick outgrew the space. So he bought an old blacksmith property, which happened to sit across the road from the Harrington Raceway, whose harness-racing season runs from mid-April through June and mid-August through October (302–398–RACE; www.harrington raceway.com). How's that for good karma?

Every year Chick's sponsors three quarter horse shows and four Standardbred sales, in addition to producing the annual Delaware Horse Expo. It's a wonder they have time to move all those horse blankets and bridles. In case you're wondering, Standardbreds are used for harness racing. Resembling Thoroughbreds, the Standardbred is more muscled, longer in the body, shorter in height, and has a larger head.

Linda met her husband (no word on whether he's as muscular as a Standardbred) while working at the (Harrington) *Journal*. After they married, she utilized her diverse skills in the family business. In the late 1970s, well before PCs and desktop publishing had entered the mainstream, Linda laid out Chick's first mail-order catalogues on the kitchen

table. Back then, she says, only one other company sold harness equipment via catalogue. "We got a bulk mail list, bulk mail permit, and 800
number" and were up and running.

Linda and Frank's colts and fillies have all been involved in the family
business at one time or another. Some still are. Today Bobby runs the
mail-order business, Jimmy works with horses and goes to shows,
daughter-in-law Robin does computer work and is a horse manager,

My kingdom for a Chick's.

Frankie is an auctioneer at tack sales, and Katie pitches in as needed. With nine grandchildren coming of age, and the elder ones already pitching in, Frank and Linda Chick won't be running "Help Wanted" ads anytime soon.

You don't need a nag, barn, or love of harness racing to go to Chick's. As I discovered early last December, it's a cool place to shop for out-of-the-ordinary holiday gifts, like boots and clothing for the whole family, and horse- and cowboy-related books, toys, and collectibles. You'll find it all at 18011 South Dupont Highway (US 13). Call (302) 398–4630 or visit www.chicksaddlery.com, where you can also shop online.

No Bull
Harrington

Delaware: It's not just for chickens anymore. Every October locals stampede to the Quillen Arena at the State Fairgrounds for the Delaware Bull Blast to watch bull riding and barrel racing. And it's not every day you can get your picture taken with a Brama bull. Buckaroos-in-training ride the miniature train and/or ponies, and everyone has a rip-snortin' good time. Leave your sandals at home, and watch where you walk.

The fairgrounds (www.delawarestatefair.com) are located on South Dupont Highway (US 13) in Harrington. For more information on the Bull Blast, call Wicked R Productions at (302) 492–3327 or go to www.wickedr.com.

The Opera House That Isn't
Smyrna

The Smyrna Opera House has served as a town hall, community center, movie theater, and library. It has been the site of lectures, concerts, children's theater, civic group meetings, auctions, and plays. Frederick Douglass spoke here in 1880, as did William Jennings Bryan in 1900 during his bid for the presidency.

But no opera has ever been sung here. Not a recitative. Not an aria. Not a single note!

The Smyrna Opera House, which is on the National Register of Historic Places, is located at 7 West South Street at the corner of Main Street. For more information call (302) 653–4236 or visit www.smyrna-operahouse.org.

Welcome to the non-opera house.

Why Are Those People Carrying Guns?
Smyrna

John Clark was a busy guy. A colonel in the Delaware militia, justice of the peace, and governor of the state from 1817 to 1820, he once lived at Clearfield Farm on the outskirts of Smyrna. The farmhouse was built by John's grandpa, Captain David Clark, in the mid-1700s.

When John Clark died in 1821, the land passed to his granddaughters. No big deal, right? Wrong. Many say the plantation was a stop on the Underground Railroad. As such, it's listed on the National Register of Historic Places. Evidence supporting the Underground Railroad claim includes a second-floor bedroom (part of the original structure) with a crawl space connecting to the attic, and a basement fireplace adjoining a dungeon. According to historians, the 1840 addition includes two doorless rooms, one with a sliding panel and the other with a 4-by-1½-foot opening. I doubt the builder had in mind a tunnel of love.

What's left for tourists to ogle.

CENTRAL DELAWARE

When I read that the house is near Duck Creek, my curiosity shifted to overdrive. All the right stuff for intrigue, illegal activity, and egress was more than enough to pique my interest. I paid little attention to the detail that the "farm" is on the grounds of the Delaware Correctional Center. If I had read the fine print, I could have saved a tankful of gas.

Driving to view this historic site, I hoped to find evidence of the Underground Railroad—at the very least, a small museum with photographs and an enthusiastic docent who would enlighten me further. One has to bob and weave to find the "plantation," 1 mile south of the intersection of Paddock Road and Smyrna Landing Road. Eureka! I spied a marker and pulled off the road. From a distance I glimpsed the Georgian–style "mansion," straight out of *The Addams Family*. Maybe *Psycho*. A heavy-duty gate separated me from the house. Then I noticed the armed guards, one led by a very large German shepherd who looked like he couldn't wait to sink his canines into my neck. As they approached, I mumbled something lame and asked if there was something I could see (other than cops and trained-to-kill dogs). Lesson learned: Never ask a question when you know the answer.

Later, at home, I connected with the writings of researcher/author K. A. Pippin, who informed me that the house is vacant except for the basement where "prison cell locks are nestled in the arch supports." Obviously Pippin had pull that I sorely lacked. She had found a splintered pillar resting against one wall, which she identified as the New Castle County Whipping Post. The last whipping, allegedly, was a thirty-year-old man who got "20 lashes for breaking and entering" in 1952.

If you want to see the marker and decrepit house, carry doggy treats. A safer way to learn more would be to visit the Clearfield Farm entry at www.harriettubman.com for more information by historian/author K.A. Pippin who, coincidentally, once worked for the Delaware Department of Corrections. Hmm . . . The plot thickens.

SLOWER DELAWARE

Milford

Prime Hook
National
Wildlife Refuge

36

113

Broadkill
Beach

18   Greenwood

18

404   404   36

13

18

Bridgeville

Milton

5

SUSSEX
COUNTY INTERIOR

1

9

23

Georgetown

404

113

Seaford

20

5   23

Woodland

9

Laurel

9

Millsboro

24

Frankford

24   24

30

24

26

Trap Pond State Park

13

Gumboro

30

Cypress
Swamp

113

1

Delmar

Selbyville

0   10 Miles

0   10 KM

SLOWER DELAWARE

Sussex County Interior

Sussex County, the southernmost Delaware county, wears two faces. One is the state's ocean beaches. (We'll get to that in the next chapter.) The other is the butt of many jokes—frequently involving chickens, pickup trucks, and double-wides.

Because of its, shall we say, down-home character, the heart of Sussex County is often referred to (*usually* with good humor) as Slower Delaware or Slower Lower Delaware. The area is a fricassee of poultry and produce farms, service businesses, and legal eagles and corporate types in Georgetown's Court of Chancery. Georgetown is the county seat and also the gullet, as it were, of the state's poultry industry.

You won't find Slower Delaware on any map. It's more a state of mind. Barefoot youngsters pedal down country lanes, and THANK A CHICKEN signs poke up like flowers (some say weeds). Produce stands, fields of freshly mowed hay, and mom-and-pop businesses abound. And chickens outnumber people. This is, after all, Perdue-land. *Buck buck buck*.

EVERYTHING YOU ALWAYS WANTED TO KNOW ABOUT CHICKENS BUT WERE AFRAID TO ASK

Fun Chicken Facts

The origins of the domestic chicken go back tens of thousands of years to the red jungle fowl of Southeast Asia.

History states that more than 4,000 years ago, Egyptians invented incubators capable of hatching as many as 10,000 chicks at a time.

Chicken is an international dish, a part of the culinary tradition of almost every nation on Earth. Some examples of a chicken dish characteristic of a country are: Spain, paella; India, chicken tandoori; France, *coq au vin;* Russia, keirnek; United States, fried chicken.

The commercial broiler chicken (chicken raised for meat) industry in the United States began in Ocean View, Delaware, in 1923.

Sussex County, Delaware, produces more broiler chickens than any other county in the United States.

The 2,500 Delmarva farm families who grow chickens own nearly 5,700 chicken houses.

Until the early 1900s, chicken was a Sunday treat, the mark of prosperity.

U.S. history records that there were chickens on the *Mayflower* with the pilgrims, that Jamestown settlers raised chickens in 1607, and that chicken was served at a Mount Vernon reception for General Lafayette.

Chicken eggs have been sent into space aboard the space shuttle and then hatched back on Earth. These "astrochix" were part of a research project studying the effects of zero gravity on growth and reproduction.

Lesser-Known Chicken Facts

Grandma was right: Chicken soup can help you feel better when you have a cold. Research from the Mayo Clinic and UCLA supports this view.

According to the *Guinness Book of World Records*, a bird named Weirdo that in 1975 weighed in at twenty-two pounds in Calaveras County, California, holds the title of the world's largest chicken.

To determine the effect of weightlessness on embryos, thirty-two fertile eggs were sent into space aboard a 1989 Discovery space shuttle mission. The results indicated that chicks hatched from "space eggs" were essentially the same as the earthbound flock.

Chicken feet (properly cleaned and inspected) are considered a food delicacy in the Far East.

A chicken, on average, has more than 8,000 feathers. However, the number of feathers will vary from one breed to another.

Americans eat about eighty pounds of chicken per person per year, an increase of more than fifty pounds per person since 1960.

CONTINUED

About 20 percent of the chickens produced in the United States are exported to countries around the world, including Russia, Japan, China, Mexico, and Canada.

A chicken can run at a speed of 25 mph.

According to the Bible, the chicken came first. The Bible states that God created the fowl on the morning of the fifth day, and later that same day he commanded the birds "to multiply upon the earth," thus producing the first egg.

A hen lays between 250 and 300 eggs per year.

A new process allows chicken feathers to be transformed into strong, absorbent fibers with the potential for use in making air filters, oil filters, and disposable diapers.

Chicken facts courtesy of Delmarva Poultry Industry, Inc. (DPI).

Calling All Pigeon Fanciers

Bridgeville

Most of us associate common street pigeons with dirt, cooing, and you better duck or wear a hat when they're around. Not so for the Del-MarVa Pigeon Fanciers. "There's no happy medium. If you like pigeons, it's like being an addict," says longtime club member Ray Merschen, a retired Bridgeville truck driver and avid pigeon fancier.

Ray has about seventy birds—they live in their own little house behind his. He's fancied pigeons since he was a kid in Philadelphia. He remembers after school, lining up around the block with other kids for feed. He got hooked early and learned much of what he knows from his father and grandfather. He cautions wannabes: "The hardest part is buying them. You have to know what you're doing." Few get into the hobby for the prize money, he says. "Most of us are in it for love."

Ray has fancied pigeons for more than fifty years.

Ray's friend Bill Terroy is another of the fifty or so members of the DelMarVa club (formed in 1980) and is also its secretary-treasurer. He and his fellow all-breed pigeon fanciers, most from Delaware, want to set the record straight about this maligned species. For openers, pigeons don't carry bird flu, Bill says. And the birds are "vaccinated, wormed, and given vitamins and the best feed," usually by the owners.

Pigeon hobbyists, clubs, and shows are big in the United States and bigger still in Europe, Pakistan, China, and Saudi Arabia, Bill says. Not just a hobby for tough, inner-city youths, as the movies would have us believe, pigeon fanciers include doctors, lawyers, corporate bigwigs, and celebrities such as the late Walt Disney, Marlon Brando, and Yul Brynner. Who knew?

There are 700 to 800 different breeds, about 200 just for show. The cost per bird runs from $5 to $50. Racers are another story: Carriers and homing pigeons compete in 100- to 1,000-mile races for big stakes and cost up to $10,000 per bird.

The DelMarVa club meets monthly. In between, they show up unannounced at each other's houses to talk shop. If you want to learn what all the cooing is about, attend one of the two shows held each year at the State Fairgrounds in Harrington (South Dupont Highway/U.S Highway 13; 302–398–3269; www.delawarestatefair.com), where the birds vie for trophies. Members also travel to other shows.

Shows? Do costumed pigeons tote little carts? Balance on a high wire? Peck "You must have been a beautiful baby . . ." on a xylophone? Actually, it's a lot like dog or horse showing. A bird can be disqualified for not measuring up—in this case, to the standards set by the National Pigeon Association's *Book of Standards*. A pigeon fancier with enough points can become a master breeder. This takes years, and to qualify you have to put in time as a judge, too. If the pigeon's weight is off, his head doesn't conform, or if a single gray feather mars an all-white standard, the bird has to find another line of work. It's that simple.

Chunkin Punkins

Bridgeville

Bridgeville is a happenin' place! The first weekend after Halloween, several thousand revelers descend on Wheatley Farms, a 1,000-acre parcel on Apple Tree Road (1 mile east of the Routes 404/18 intersection), for the World Championship Punkin Chunkin (302–684–8196; www.punkin chunkin.com). You haven't lived if you haven't yet seen people hurling giant pumpkins from homemade catapults that Rube Goldberg would have been proud to claim.

A local tradition for more than twenty years, in 2006 the festival lost its lease in Millsboro (owing to developers with bigger ideas for the land than squashed squash). Bridgeville stepped in and now rents the land to the festival for $1.

Gourds line up for a smashing finish at this event.

Participants with the right stuff (some spend *months* crafting their machines) fling their Halloween gourds a mile or more. Some of the categories for adult and youth entries include Air, Catapult, Trebuchet, Human Power, Centrifugal, and Theatrical. This is serious stuff. If you don't believe me, take a look at the list of "Official Classes and Rules." For example, "Any machine that shoots out of the field of play will be allowed three hours to have spotters locate Pumpkin. The field of play is defined as not being in the woods. If it is spotted up to the wood line it is considered in the field. If in the field of play you will not need the three hours location time."

During three days of festivities, there's live entertainment, a pumpkin-cooking contest, and plenty of food. (Please note, "All times are Sussex County time which is within an hour of the advertised times.") Y'all come. You are welcome to mimic the many who wear orange to the event. But take care—you could be mistaken for a pumpkin and end up in a sling.

Sling That Scrapple

Bridgeville

Next to Punkin Chunkin, swatting flies, and watching the cars inch hood-to-fender to the ocean, the biggest event in Bridgeville is the annual Apple Scrapple Festival (www.applescrapple.com) held in October. Like all good festivals and fairs, it centers around food. I'll tip my fork to that. An all-you-can-eat breakfast Saturday is worth the drive alone. At the festival you can have apples pied, fried, sauced, and frittered. Take that, Johnny Appleseed. A Delaware friend says she packs on three pounds every October—and that's before Halloween.

In case you didn't know, local apples are a leading industry in the First State, and RAPA Scrapple (www.rapascrapple.com) has been doing biz in Bridgeville since 1926. Scrapple is less familiar to some. For many southerners, and residents of Pennsylvania and Delaware, it's a must-have. According to the Gospel of Scrapple, Dutch settlers in the seventeenth and eighteenth centuries made their home in the Delaware River valley. Known for their *thriftiness* (how's that for a polite euphemism?), the burghers created scrapple from leftovers—the bits of pork ("scraps") left in the iron kettle after they had, um, porked out. Scrapple's die-hard fans go into paroxysms of delight at the mere mention of the dish. I say, try it. But do yourself a favor—don't ask what's in it until after you've eaten some.

But I digress. At the Apple Scrapple Festival you can do more than stuff your face. In addition to carnival games, music, tractor pulls, and dancing, the top activities include the Mayor's Scrapple Sling (I am not making this up), open to all Sussex County mayors. The winner is designated the "King of Sling." For the Scrapple Chunkin, contestants hurl scrapple packages from catapults. As you can see, catapults are big business around here.

If you want to make scrapple at home, here's a general recipe I culled from the dozen or so I reviewed (you'll have to adapt the ingredients to your own taste). Take some pork, but not your lean bacon or ham. Which parts you use is up to you—any combination of pigs' knuckles, boneless cooked pork loin, or a whole hog head and innards (including eyes, heart, liver, and bladder) will do. Cook it down in a very big pot. Still with me? Add salt, pepper, seasonings (usually thyme or sage or both), cornmeal, and flour till you have mush. Bake the mush in a loaf pan. Allow to cool. Slice, dust with flour, and pan fry in butter, vegetable oil, or bacon fat. Don't have your cholesterol checked for at least six months.

Twofer the Price of One
Delmar

The 1,000 or so residents living in the 19940 zip code may be hard-pressed to choose sides. And they may be prey to more than their share of identity crises. Who could blame them? The town, in the southwestern corner of the state, straddles the Mason-Dixon line and the Delaware–Maryland border. No wonder it's known as "The Little Town That's Too Big For One State."

Founded in 1859, and rebuilt in the early twentieth century after fires swept through, Delmar flourished for many years as the "Strawberry Capital of the Nation," owing to the efforts of local farmers. Today it's a destination for car-racing enthusiasts who fill the US 13 Dragway and Delaware International Speedway (302–875–1911; www.delaware racing.com) to cheer their favorite drivers.

Peachy Keen
Frankford

Peach lovers in search of a uniquely Delaware experience should mark their July and August calendars. Picking fruit at Bennett Orchards on Route 20 in Frankford (302–732–3358; www.bennettorchards.com) is one of life's—and summer's—sweeter experiences.

"We're the only pick-your-own-peaches orchard in Delaware," says Carrie Bennett. "We grow twenty varieties of yellow and rare white peaches, plus nectarines." (Who knew there were so many varieties? I thought there were four: fresh, canned, frozen, and schnapps.) Carrie urges potential peach pickers to call first because the already short season is also prey to the whims of Mother Nature. A drought, too much rain, or a cold snap can take a toll and speed or delay the ripening. The orchard supplies containers and asks pickers to return them in exchange for a free pound of peaches on their next visit. While there's a ten-pound minimum, you'll probably devour that before you leave the field.

The orchard has been in the Bennett family for five generations, and the sixth generation is in training. In the 1780s the land was the site of a gristmill and sawmills. The original farmhouse (circa 1850s) stands on the property. The Bennetts planted their first peach tree in 1982 and show no signs of slowing down.

For information on Delaware's other seventy-five or so farm markets, go to www.state.de.us/deptagri.

All Dolled Up
Georgetown

Elsie Steele Williams—what a doll! The wife of U.S. senator John Williams ("Honest John," who served four terms and five presidents), of Millsboro, bequeathed her large doll collection to Del Tech in 1990. An extension of her interests and well-traveled life, the dolls paint a picture of twentieth-century fashions, mores, and social history.

The centerpiece of the Williams exhibit, the Brides of America series, all Danbury Mint exclusives, might well be called Here Come the Brides. For example, as a bride of the 1940s, Dorothy (maybe she was named for *The Wizard of Oz*'s Dorothy?) wears an ivory satin, full-length gown with satin brocade trim. From Williams's handwritten notes we learn that "the long veil was probably borrowed because of the scarcity of materials" during World War II.

Brides aside, there are dolls in native dress from Europe, the Philippines, the Caribbean, and South America donated by globe-trotting Anna Teel, and a collection of teacher dolls donated by Kathryn Megyri, a Maryland high school English teacher. Among the well-preserved antiques are early twentieth-century German– and French–made dolls with bisque heads.

Here come the brides.

This is definitely worth a stop on your way to or from the beach—the Elsie Williams Doll Collection is a real gem. It's located in the Stephen J. Betze Library, Delaware Technical & Community College, Owens Campus, Route 18, Georgetown. Call (302) 856–9033 for more information.

Atocha So
Georgetown

In the unlikely setting of a community college (down the hall from the Elsie Williams Doll Collection) lies the Treasures of the Sea exhibit (Stephen J. Betze Library, Delaware Tech, Route 18; 302–856–5700; www.treasuresofthesea.org). Tucked away between the library and restrooms are artifacts recovered by Mel Fisher from the Spanish galleon *Nuestra Señora de Atocha.*

The *Atocha,* you may recall, sank in a hurricane off the Florida Keys in 1622. The ship had been on its way back to Spain after picking up gold, silver, and precious gems in Cuba and South America, when the storm cut short its voyage by several thousand miles. After breaking up on a coral reef, the ship sank within minutes in 50 feet of water (and everyone missed karaoke night and the midnight buffet). Despite repeated attempts, the Spanish failed to locate the ship. *Es una lástima!*

More than 300 years later, along came treasure hunter Mel Fisher who, subsidized by a team of investors, searched for the sunken ship for 20 years. In 1985 he finally found what he was looking for (unlike Bono, who still hasn't found what he's looking for). Of course, the good ole U.S. government had to weigh in, claiming title to the booty. Then Florida (pre–Jeb Bush) got into the act and seized some small-potato items that Fisher had recovered *before* the BIG haul. Eight years of litigation later, the Supreme Court decided in Fisher's favor. Perseverance pays. Way to go, Mel.

So how did some of the treasure land in Georgetown, of all places? Well, Delaware chicken maven Frank ("It takes a tough man to make a tender chicken") Perdue and some other well-feathered Delaware businessmen invested in Fisher's recovery efforts—otherwise know as Diving for Dollars. In exchange for the gold the local investors had given Fisher, they got some back. Perdue then donated some of his take to the exhibit, providing a golden opportunity for all involved.

Burying the Hatchet
Georgetown

Sussex County has the unique distinction of being the only county in the nation (as far as we know) to celebrate the end of election season every two years. They call it Return Day. One wonders why the practice is not widely adapted elsewhere—if only to celebrate the end of such sludge-slinging as that which accompanied the 2006 midterms. Return Day's roots may reach as far back as 1792, a year after the county seat moved from Lewes to Georgetown. In olden times, voters historically returned to the courthouse to hear the election results. OK, now that we have that squared away . . .

On the Thursday following the Tuesday election, the winning and losing candidates ride side-by-side in horse-drawn carriages and antique cars to demonstrate that they've put aside any hard feelings—for a day, at least. After parading through the streets of Georgetown, they rendezvous in front of the historic 1837 courthouse on the circle. From the balcony a town crier announces the tallies, re-creating a practice begun in the early nineteenth century when the sheriff would announce the election results to the citizens of the county's "hundreds" (similar to today's townships). Next on the agenda, the local pols bury a tomahawk in a glass "casket" filled with beach sand. Partisanship is forgotten as Republicans, Democrats, and Independents dig into the same slow-cooked beef barbecue and fraternize throughout the evening. Music, food, and craft booths round out the festivities.

You don't have to be a pol—or even a VIP or Delaware resident—to attend. The events begin Wednesday afternoon (one day postelection) and run through Thursday, and all are open to the general public. For more information call (302) 855–0711 or visit www.returnday.org.

GAS POWER

In late 2006 state and energy officials announced that no fewer than seven generators will convert Delaware-produced gas (methane) from decomposing waste into energy. Methane, you may recall from Al Gore's documentary, contributes to the greenhouse effect that is melting the polar ice cap and may very well spell the end of life on Earth as we've known it. So turning gas into something useful is a good thing indeed!

In its unrenewed state, the gas in question resides in Kent and Sussex County garbage landfills that are owned and operated by the Delaware Solid Waste Authority (DSWA). Previously, in a variation of the light-the-match/blue flame trick, the methane had been burned in a flare. The new gas-converting generators are said to produce 7.4 megawatts of power, enough to provide electricity for about 4,500 homes. That's a lot of baked beans to fire up plasma-screen TVs and PCs.

One can't help wondering if the date—mere days after Thanksgiving, no doubt the most gaseous of all holidays—played a role in the timing of the announcement. No further word on whether a means has been found to infuse the gas with air freshener before it electrifies area homes. Maybe the power company will include a book of matches with every consumer's monthly bill.

Let's hear it for renewable energy!

Pollo, Si!

Georgetown

In the mid-1990s a large wave of Guatemalans came to Slower Delaware to work in Sussex County's poultry processing plants. This is not a new story of emigrants coming to a new country to work for slave wages. Who else wants to work for $8 an hour to eviscerate chickens? (In the interest of fairness, following a probationary period, the pay jumps to a whopping $9.70.)

At first the workers crammed into rundown houses in the down-on-its-heels Kimmeytown section of Georgetown. Where else would they live? In a McMansion on the "right" side of the tracks? As you might imagine, some old-timers were less than thrilled with their new neighbors. (A *New Yorker* writer once dubbed Sussex County "the northernmost county of Mississippi.") Perhaps someone told the locals, "Get over it!" because relations have improved for the most part. Heck, the locals don't want to spend their days fingering chicken innards. They're glad somebody else is doing the dirty work.

Little more than a decade after the first influx of Guatemalan workers arrived, Kimmeytown, near the old railroad depot, has a new face. The workers' families have joined them. They bought old properties, fixed them up, and moved in. They've opened new businesses like the large Mercado (15 Layton Avenue; 302–856–6081), a transcultural market that merits a visit, across from the railroad tracks. *Los niños* score high (higher than their Anglo counterparts) on standardized tests at the local elementary school, which, by the way, has received the U.S. Department of Education's National Blue Ribbon School Award. And these days some poultry processing plants are paying more than lip service to Diversity Day.

SLOWER DELAWARE

Like yin and yang, with change come challenges. Two Spanish-speaking officers have joined the Georgetown police force, and Tuesday is Spanish arraignment night in the local court.

Georgetown's Statue of Liberty.

FRY IT UP CRISP

The *original* world's largest frying pan—a whopping 10 feet in diameter—holds enough breasts, thighs, and legs to satisfy Paul Bunyan (or Hugh Hefner). The pan served as a goodwill—and good fowl—ambassador for the tristate Delmarva Chicken Festival (www.dpichicken.org) from 1950 to 1988. When it retired from active duty, more than a hundred tons of chicken had crisped in the 650-pound, 8-inch-deep pan. The handle alone weighed eight pounds.

Mumford Sheet Metal Works of Selbyville made the original, and God bless 'em, when the original got plum worn out, they produced a duplicate in 1988. Like its predecessor, Pan II is divided into four sections, mounted on concrete blocks, and capable of turning out 800 pounds of fried chicken at a time—and that ain't chicken feed.

Because Delaware, Maryland, and Virginia are such good buds and copartner the festival, they take turns hosting it. While chowing down on chicken served several ways, french fries, baked goods (gotta have some sweets), and other healthful treats, you can watch a parade, enjoy music, and take part in chicken-related entertainment.

If you'd like to fix Delaware–style fried chicken for your family some Sunday, the Delmarva Poultry Industry, Inc., in Georgetown generously shared the ingredients you'll need:

8,000 pieces of chicken

375 pounds of flour

60 pounds of salt

30 pounds of pepper

30 pounds of paprika

180 gallons of cooking oil

(NOTE: This makes enough for the two-day festival.)

Maybe you have a favorite chicken recipe? Why not enter it in the annual National Chicken Cooking Contest (www.eatchicken .com)? What've you got to lose? You might win the grand prize of $100,000.

If you can't make the annual festival, visit the original pan at the Delaware History Museum, located in a former Woolworth's in Wilmington (504 Market Street; 302–656–0637; www.hsd.org). Head for the Distinctively Delaware exhibit.

Holds enough breasts and thighs for *Playboy*.

Yes, There's a Doctor in the House
Georgetown

You could do worse than to be a sick chicken in Delaware. The Poultry Diagnostic Center on Route 9 in Georgetown employs a staff of sophisticated chicken-savvy researchers and diagnosticians who spend their days heading off and treating flu and infection outbreaks.

The staff is known and recognized worldwide for keeping a*breast* (a little chicken humor there) of the latest developments affecting the area's broiler industry. Besides studying up to 3,000 blood samples per month in the serology lab, the researchers have a *leg* up on everybody else as to the effects of water, soil, and other environmental factors on local fowl.

So don't be surprised if, while driving past Sussex County poultry farms, you hear the chickens vocalizing their appreciation as a collective *thigh* of relief.

Farming Alpacas in Chickenland
Greenwood

Next time you're shopping for alpacas—or maybe you want to meet one of these curious-looking creatures up close and personal—make an appointment to visit Long Meadow Farm in Greenwood (302–349–0830; www.delawarealpacas.com). Amy Robb; her husband, Doug, a civil engineer; and their fifty kids (forty-eight alpacas and two bipeds, Rachel and Tanner) call Long Meadow home.

An animal lover with a biology degree who once considered a career as a veterinarian, Amy grew up on a farm with sheep and a pony. When her daughter was born, Amy sought animals who'd be "gentle with kids." That meant "no nasty rams," she says. Bingo!

A face only a mother could love.

Often confused with llamas, a close relative, Amy explains that "the alpaca is smaller and gentler and has a finer fleece. They're fiber rather than pack animals." The babies sometimes chase her kids like puppies do, she says, "and you can tell them [the alpacas] apart by their personality." Any downside? They don't like Delaware's summer heat and humidity. (Welcome to the club!) To keep them comfortable, the Robbs "turn fans on in the summer and hose them down."

There's a strong national market for alpacas, Amy says. Long Meadow alpacas have moved as far away as Texas. Jeez, if they thought Delaware was hot . . .

Finger-Lickin' Fantastic
Greenwood

If you're headed through Delaware on a Friday, Saturday, or Sunday (Monday, too, on holiday weekends) April through October, take a detour and follow your nose to the Greenwood Volunteer Fire Co. on US 13 (between the north- and southbound lanes, just south of the Route 16 intersection; 302–349–4529). Then roll up your sleeves and tear into succulent, flavorful, falling-off-the-bone BBQ chicken. Guaranteed, you'll thank me.

A local tradition for more than forty-five years, this may well be the *sine qua non* of PR for Delaware's $500-million-a-year poultry industry and for Sussex County, which is No. 1 among U.S. counties in broiler chicken production. Volunteers from VFW Post 7478 and the Greenwood fire company split the chickens and the season, sharing the responsibility for turning and basting the birds on the 45-foot steel-plated pit. We begged and pleaded for the secret-sauce recipe. This is what we squeezed from the cooks: "It's oil, cider vinegar, salt, pepper, seasonings, and [mumbling]." Unlike cloying thick sauces that often mask the bird's flavor, this one enhances it.

SLOWER DELAWARE

The best way to eat this bird? Like a present-day Henry VIII—with the utensils at the end of your arms. For $6 you get half a chicken or two leg quarters, pickle slices, a potato roll (for sopping the juice), and a small bag of potato chips. Can you beat it? One of the nice volunteers behind the counter will pack it to go, if you like. But why wait? Park your tail feathers at a picnic table and have at it.

So you don't miss out on this singular Delaware experience, I recommend getting there early during July and August. The chickens start flying off the pit and into hungry customers' mouths around 9:00 A.M., often selling out by 3:00 or 4:00 P.M. The early bird may get the worm elsewhere; here the early diner gets the bird.

Move over, Colonel Sanders.

HOME IMPROVEMENTS

In an act of unprecedented generosity (and necessity), in June 2006 the U.S. Department of Agriculture gave the Delmarva Poultry Industry, Inc. (representing the industry in all three states) $52,700 to plant trees around chicken houses. Believe me, beautification was not at the heart of this initiative. The so-called VEBs (Vegetative Environmental Buffers) are intended to improve the air quality around poultry farms. Hey, it can only get better. If you've ever driven through the area (even with windows closed) on a hot day, you know what I'm talking about. Someone would make a killing selling air-freshener around here.

It is hoped that the trees will reduce "the movement of poultry house dust, feathers, odors, and gases to neighboring properties," among other things. Can mini-Jacuzzis and swimming pools be far behind? In the future let's hope that those in power do more about the chicken-related runoff into Delaware's streams and rivers.

Trees? Maybe next year they'll put in a pool.

Fowls Foul Ticks

Gumboro

Bill Stevenson farms on Good Flocking Way (no, I didn't make that up), about 8 miles west of Millsboro. Overshoot it a few yards, and you'll land in Maryland. From October through June, Bill sells his free-range eggs at his farm (well, not *his* eggs; they are from his hens). "On a good day" they don't lay enough to keep Bill in chicken feed, so he also sells guinea fowls to a loyal following.

Trade them for what's behind the curtain? Not on your life.

Why guinea fowls? Bill says they control the nasty ticks that carry Lyme disease. Who'da thunk it? Ticks are arachnids, not insects, Bill explains. The guinea fowls also have a taste for pesky insects, providing a safe alternative to toxic pesticides. He has "about seventy guinea fowls in my keepers flock, twenty more young ones for sale," and sells them individually. Don't they get lonesome? Bill says it's one at a time because "until they can make the *buck-wheat* sound that identifies a female, there is no foolproof way to sex them." Too much information, Bill.

Saturday mornings July through September, Bill sells his eggs at the Historic Lewes Farmers Market (Third and Ship Carpenter Streets in Lewes), usually with his feathered friends in tow. Hey, chickens like to get out and take a road trip every now and again, too, you know. Affable birds *all*, they enjoy the spotlight and will pose for your digital.

I'm a realist: I know you'll probably move through life without visiting Bill. But you may want to call and say hello (302–238–7809). When he's unavailable, the chickens answer. *Buck buck buck buck. Nobody here but us chickens. We're here while Bill's away, keeping an eye on things. Don't give up, he'll be back. We'll give him the message . . .*

A Bargain Is a Bargain Is a . . .
Laurel

For more than a quarter century, bargain hunters have been swarming to Bargain Bill's flea market in Laurel every Friday, Saturday, and Sunday. No less an authority than *Good Housekeeping* has approved Bargain Bill's, proclaiming it one of the top fifty flea markets in the United States.

Granted, it can be slow and lackluster inside, especially on a Friday. But out back scores of tables groan under the weight of goods on Saturday and Sunday. Here's a sampling of what I found in a recent sweep:

Good Housekeeping approves.

- Sequin cinch belt for $2.98 (How could I deny myself?)
- Do-rag with skull and flames (Everyone needs at least two.)
- Hot dogs, pizza, fresh-squeezed lemonade (Satisfying the basic food groups.)
- Acrylic bath tubs (Couldn't squeeze one into the two-door Honda.)
- Asian groceries (Priced well; whip out your wok.)
- Porcelain bust of James Dean ($75, but I could have had it for $50.)
- Wigs (You can get one in every color of the psychedelic rainbow.)
- Jewelry (The good, the bad, and the ugly.)
- DVDs (Got some for the kids.)
- A tailor (They couldn't lengthen my high-waters while I waited.)
- Lottery tickets (I'd rather spend $ on bargains.)
- Postcards ("Wish you were here." Not.)
- A sign: CHEESY SLEEZY [sic] SOUVENIRS (You gotta love it!)

Bargain Bill's is located off US 13 at 10912 County Seat Highway. For more information call (302) 875–9958.

SLOWER DELAWARE

Bayou North

Laurel

The *northernmost* stands of bald cypress trees on the Atlantic coast are about 5 miles east of Laurel at Trap Pond State Park (33587 Baldcypress Lane; 302–875–05153; www.destateparks.com). If you didn't know better, you'd swear you were in Louisiana.

The park is open year-round dawn to dusk and offers boat rentals in summer. It's located in the biologically diverse, dam-free (as opposed to *damn free*) Nanticoke River watershed. Besides being a super place for anglers, the river is fished commercially—for American shad, blueback herring (is that with or without the sour cream and onions?), alewife, catfish, striped bass (rockfish), white perch, and other species, according to the Delaware Department of Natural Resources.

If you're into birding, fly on over. The area is known for having the highest concentration of bald eagles in the northeastern United States.

Captain, My Captain

Laurel

During his exploration of the area back in 1607, Captain John Smith (the guy with the ruffled collar, tickly beard, and big ego who most likely invented the myth about getting it on with Pocahontas) came as far as Broad Creek in Laurel. A 2007 reenactment celebrating the 400th anniversary of his arrival at the Laurel landing on May 29—complete with a peace-pipe offering—is a blast from the past. Not widely known is why Smith and his buddies, calling themselves the Virginia Company, ended up in Jamestown.

109

You won't find this in the history books, and their ancestors will likely deny it, so don't bother asking. It pains me to dispel a popular myth, but the Virginia Company was not exploring the region with an eye toward settling. Oh no. The guys were on their way to a golf outing at the Homestead. They got lost and wouldn't stop to ask for directions. And that's how they found Jamestown.

Down by the Old Mill Stream
Milford

Once upon a time, Delaware had 130 millponds, a number that has dwindled in recent years to 60. Today Abbott's Mill (15411 Abbott's Pond Road; 302–422–0847; www.delawarenaturesociety.org) is the only surviving millpond in the state with a standing mill and working machinery. Until it shut down in 1960, Abbott's Mill produced high-quality flour, buckwheat, and cornmeal. A water turbine replaced the wooden water wheel in the late nineteenth century.

While the nature center is open daily, the mill is not. But several times a year the public can attend special programs that include a tour of the gristmill. Talk about a living-history experience! The chutes, buhr stones, shafts and pulleys, the sheller, and grinders in the two-story building are something to see. Today's "technology" seems less hotsy-totsy by comparison. Staff like Jason Beale and Elliott Workman are so knowledgeable—about the mill's workings, as well as the local flora and fauna—that it's downright scary.

One of the mill-related family events tracks the interaction of plants and waterpower and culminates in a pancake breakfast. (Food? Did someone mention food?) Participants also learn how to tap a maple tree for syrup. Hey, what are pancakes without syrup? During special mill tours, visitors see the grindstone—4 feet across and tipping the scale at one ton—that used to grind corn and wheat. In days of yore the miller had to recut grooves in the stone every two to three days to keep it in top shape. What a fun job that must have been!

Don't file your nails with this.

Just Ducky
Milford

You could have knocked Richard C. Clifton over with a feather—a duck feather, that is. In October 2006 the self-taught wildlife artist and gallery owner learned that he had won the 2006 Federal Duck Stamp Art Contest, the nation's most prestigious contest of its kind, for his

Let's blow this pond and head south.

SLOWER DELAWARE

acrylic of a male and female ring-necked duck. His painting beat out 296 entries from 49 states. The stamp, on sale July 1, 2007, raises awareness and funds for the National Wildlife Refuge System's wetland habitat acquisition.

Clifton's work has appeared on other wildlife stamps, and he had entered this contest several times before, but winning the big kahuna was a first. "Some artists keep count; I don't," says the self-effacing Clifton. If you'd like to see what else he does, you may visit the artist by appointment at his Milford gallery/studio, Gallery at Eastwind, 9397 Cods Road; call (302) 684–4747.

Ladybug, Ladybug . . .
Milford

In 1974 Millie Rust-Brown's second-grade pupils at Lulu Ross Elementary School decided Delaware needed a state bug. After much discussion, the kids voted for the ladybug—which won big over the mosquito and cricket. The kids wrote then-governor Sherman Tribbett who, duly impressed, visited the school and suggested how the second-graders could make their wish a reality.

With the help of local high schoolers, the kids learned about the democratic process, sought support from other school districts, and got a bill introduced into the legislature. On a page missing from most history books, Rep. Lewis B. Harrington introduced House Bill No. 667 in the House of Representatives on March 9, 1974. After additional campaigning (ladybug badges and clothing, and appearances at political dinners), the kids were invited to Legislative Hall on April 25. Dressed as ladybugs and carrying posters, the children marched around the hall. Not even the crustiest pol could resist. The vote was unanimous, and the governor signed the bill on the back of a student dressed in—what else?—a ladybug costume.

The LadyBug Shop at 19 West Front Street (302–422–5470; www.ladybug-shop.com) celebrates the students' efforts and the state bug with a collection of endearing red-and-black merchandise—toys, books, clothing, jewelry, and accessories. When in Milford, show your solidarity for the ladybug with a visit to its namesake shop!

Paying homage to the state bug.

IDENTITY CRISIS

The Mispillion (pronounced *Miss-PILL-yun*) River flows gracefully through Milford's historic downtown area, establishing the boundary between Kent and Sussex Counties. Take a stroll along the Riverwalk, and see if you can figure out which county you're in.

One side's Kent, the other is Sussex.

Heavy Metal
Millsboro

From April to the end of October, you'll find Judy and Lou Hagen in the truck they share, hauling produce to Michigan, Ohio, North Carolina, Alabama, and Florida. When they return to Delaware sometime before Halloween, they don't veg in their recliners, turn on the tube, and clip coupons until the following spring. No siree. Before the rig's engine has cooled, they're in their garage studio, 2nd Time Designs (302–945–3988; www.2ndtimedesigns.com; studio visits by appointment), putting together whimsical metal sculptures and painting them in a rainbow palette.

It all started in 1999, Judy says. "We saw some wacky stuff in front of a 7-Eleven in Georgia and took pictures. I thought to myself, I can do better." Although they had always made small stuff for themselves and as gifts, both Judy and Lou are self-taught. They forage until they find a scrap or castoff that dictates where the design will go. So far, business has come via word of mouth and their membership in Delaware By Hand (www.delawarebyhand.org), a consortium of talented local artisans.

Featured in October 2006 on HGTV's *Offbeat America,* Judy and Lou are currently working on something for Baltimore's Visionary Arts Museum. Examples of their work, like the oversize fisherman reeling in his catch, decorate their lawn about 5 miles east of Millsboro, at 26380 John Williams Highway (Route 24). I dare you to drive by without stopping to snap photos.

Landing the big one.

Powwow Packs Pow and Wow—and How

Millsboro

Every second weekend in September, Nanticokes ("people of the tide-waters"), along with members of other tribes from as far away as Canada, gather to celebrate and preserve their rich heritage at the award-winning Nanticoke Powwow, held just west of the Nanticoke Indian Museum on John J. Williams Highway (Route 24).

From the Algonquian *pauwau,* powwow can refer to "any gathering of native people." Healing and driving away negative energy are integral to powwows. And dancing is the heart of the powwow, with the drum providing the heartbeat. Before you put on your dancin' shoes, however, you should know that dancing is restricted to members of the tribe. But no one can stop you from moving in place, and most visitors are hard-pressed to stand still. For sheer spectacle, you'd have to travel to Radio City Music Hall to top the Grand Entry procession of dancers in native dress, the presentation of flags, dancing and music, lighting of the peace pipe, storytelling, and invocations to the Great Spirit.

Tribal history lives here.

You certainly don't have to go native to fill up on delicious Indian fry bread, Indian–style tacos, and more mainstream eats. This is also a swell opportunity to pick up crafts, pottery, paintings, jewelry, and clothing. Kids can have their faces painted. (They're dirty anyway, so why not?) You'd do well to bring a lawn chair.

The Nanticoke Indian Museum, located in a former one-room school for Nanticoke children, always merits a visit—for its artifacts (arrowheads, spears, and pottery), beadwork and crafts, art, research library, and to meet museum guide Patience ("Pat") Harmon, a wealth of information with the right pedigree for the job. The museum is located at John J. Williams Highway (Route 24) and Oak Orchard Road (Route 5). For more information about both the powwow and the museum, call (302) 945–7022 or log on to www.nanticokeindians.org.

Holly Capital of the World
Milton

Once upon a time, boys and girls, about one hundred years ago, Milton supplied the entire nation and beyond with holly wreaths from Delaware's state tree, *Ilex opaca*. A Milton fertilizer salesman (bet he was a joy to be around), Charles C. Jones Sr., known as "Jones, the Holly Wreath Man," initiated the boom that put Milton on the map as the leading exporter of holly worldwide.

Are you old enough to remember the black-and-white newsreels that ran before main features in the days before multiplexes? Well, some of these films immortalized Milton, showing locals who "grew, clipped, formed, and shipped" the holiday decorations culled from the tree. And if you drive through Milton today, you will see some beautiful examples of the state tree, some soaring 60 feet into the Slower Delaware sky.

Hopped-up Family

Milton

Like other college students the world over, Sam Calagione sought beer that was cheap and plentiful. And, like many an undergrad, he learned about home brewing. Postgraduation, while he was figuring out what to do with the rest of his life, he bartended in New York City and studied creative writing—a dead-end career, if ever there was one. His interest in home brewing grew and, gutsy guy that he was, he decided to take a stab at producing microbrewed beer. One can only imagine how thrilled his family was with that news. Even after several banks dissed him, Sam persevered. After some family and friends put their money where their mouths are, he finally got a bank loan.

In 1995 Sam opened Dogfish Head Brewings & Eats in Rehoboth Beach. At Dogfish Head Craft Brewery (named for a peninsula in Maine where his family vacationed, "a place of shelter"), he began brewing in a ten-gallon barrel that the UPS man delivered. The "smallest brewery in the U.S." had been born. Before long Dogfish had seven barrels. The beer caught on, mostly by word of mouth (no pun intended), and before you could say, "Get me a cold one," Dogfish Head had leased 5,000 square feet in nearby Lewes.

In the truth-is-stranger-than-fiction category, the family of Sam's wife, Mariah, had once owned but later sold the Draper-King Cole cannery in Milton. The family of Sam's wife Mariah bought it (again) in 2002. With Mariah as VP, Sam set up shop there with thirty barrels. Today the state-of-the-art operation has 150 barrels producing close to forty kinds of beer—several ales, stouts, Lawnmower Light, limited editions, seasonals like Punkin Ale, brewpub exclusives, and—*ta-da!*—Blue Hen Vodka. The brewery sends out six to eight loaded trucks per day to destinations as far away as Portland (Oregon) and Seattle. Each

Brewmaster breaks for a Raison D'Extra.

truck holds twenty-two pallets, sixty cases per pallet. You do the math. And while you're up, get me a Dogfish Head 60 Minute IPA.

Dogfish Head Craft Brewery is located at 6 Cannery Village Center in Milton, and tours are available every Monday, Wednesday, and Friday at 3:00 P.M. For more information call (302) 684–1000, or you can visit www.dogfish .com.

Ye Olde Hardware Store
Seaford

Stepping into Burton Bros. (407 High Street, 302–629–8595), I can't help wondering how many other feet have crossed the threshold since 1893, the year the hardware store opened its doors. Just think, while the help was stocking the shelves, Grover Cleveland lived at 1600 Pennsylvania Avenue and the Gibson Girl was hot.

The store's pressed tin ceiling, original counters, and plank floors are beyond impressive. Then you spy the nuts, bolts, and screws in tarnished but serviceable bins that have been in use for more than a century. In our throwaway culture, it's the stuff of science fiction. Old—really old—store calendars hang from the walls. Upstairs is an Atwater Kent radio, and next to it, an all-brass cash register that can ring up a sale all the way to $3.

Ah, for the good old days.

Today customers come in to purchase paints, pipes, filters, and such and stay to swap stories, inquire after ailing relatives, and share a laugh with the sales staff. Service is brisk but never rushed, and always cordial.

The Burtons sold the business to the Marvel family in 1954. Today third-generation Marvels—Ron and his brother Richard ("Ric")—run it under the Burton name. "I started here in 1971," Ron says. "My grandfather, Charles Marvel, worked here, then my father, Sherwood." The business has been in the hands of only two families for more than 110 years—not a bad track record.

Despite their commitments to the business and to family, Ron and Ric have been active in the Seaford Volunteer Fire Department for more than thirty years. If you ask real nice, and he's not too busy, Ron will take you across the street to see the gleaming white historic (1921) fire engine. She's a spit-and-polished beauty that the fire department brings out for Christmas and firemen's festival parades.

Monsterville
Selbyville

As far back as the 1920s, as the story goes (and it goes plenty), some coon hunters in the Great Cypress Swamp west of Fenwick Island (Route 54 and U.S. Highway 113) heard screaming. They reported something chasing them, something so large that its footfalls snapped branches. Locals speculated that it might have been a black bear. For years there were rumors, sightings, whispers, and innuendo. (Reminds me of E!) The legend grew, and next thing you know, Delaware had its own version of Bigfoot and the Loch Ness Monster.

Fast forward to the 1960s. The rumors persisted. Some claimed that they'd captured the so-called Selbyville Swamp Monster on their pre-digital cameras. He was said to be tall, hairy, and possessing breath most foul. Picture Chubaka with a 'tude and halitosis—or your worst Match.com nightmare.

For decades fear and trepidation filled anyone entering the swamp, especially after dark. And then the monster revealed himself. It seems the haunting had been programmed, begun as a marketing ploy. Fred Stevens of Selbyville (the town historian and a fourth-generation resident) says the editor of the now defunct *Delmarva News* glimpsed him in Selbyville's annual Halloween parade—"1962 or '63," Fred recalls—and had an *aha!* moment. "He thought it would boost circulation," Fred says. Fred wore a mask, his aunt's ratty old raccoon coat, and a pair of pants he had dragged behind his truck to season them. Some swamp monster! The photos, of course, were all posed. When they hit the paper, they fueled the frenzy and boosted circulation for a spell. (The paper went out of business in 1990.)

In the 1980s, Fred says, *Strange* magazine (also now defunct) came knocking. In true show-biz fashion, Fred handed over the old costume to his son, who led the journalists on a tour of the Swamp Monster's old stomping grounds. Why didn't Fred go and relive a piece of his golden past? "I sent my son because I weigh 230 pounds. I couldn't get into the clothes now."

Crossing Nanticoke
Woodland

Drive onto the cable-run Woodland Ferry (Woodland Road, about 4.8 miles—or 10 minutes—west of Seaford) and, in the time it takes to turn off your ignition and get out of your car, you'll have arrived at your destination. That's because the river is only slightly wider than the ferry's length! Though it's billed as a three-car ferry, I wouldn't want to be the third.

SLOWER DELAWARE

James Cannon began ferry service here in the 1740s, and it stayed in the family for close to a century. Then the county stepped in and legislated for "a public ferry across the Nanticoke River . . . teams, wagons, and carriages, shall be transported . . . between sunrise and sunset, free of charge." DelDOT took over in 1935 and has operated the ferry ever since. It runs from 6:00 A.M. to 8:00 P.M. in summer, 6:00 A.M. to 6:00 P.M. in winter.

One of the oldest ferries in the country, it once carried entrepreneurial Marylander Patty Cannon between her home state and Delaware. It is said that her business—transporting kidnapped slaves and free blacks to Georgia for resale—made her a frequent rider.

Plans for a new, larger ferry are in the works. I sure hope they don't have in mind a huge paddle wheeler. Every September a festival celebrates the ferry and its history; call the Woodland Ferry Association at (302) 629–8077 or 628–0825 for details.

No time (or room) for walking the deck.

BEACHES

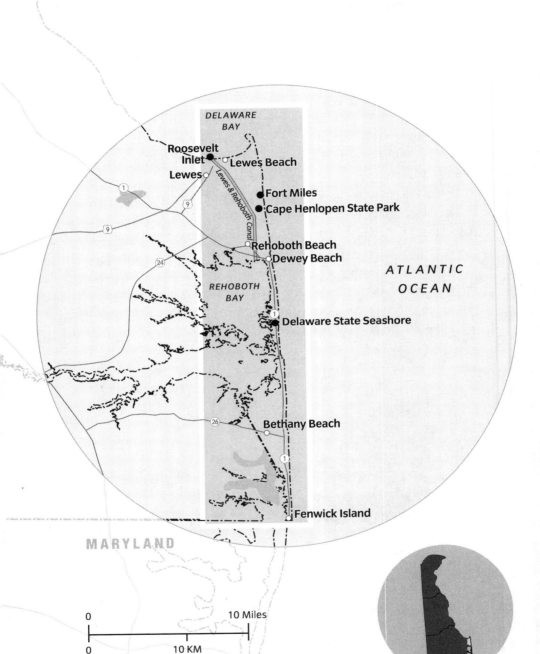

DELAWARE BAY

Roosevelt Inlet
Lewes Beach
Lewes

Lewes & Rehoboth Canal

Fort Miles
Cape Henlopen State Park

Rehoboth Beach
Dewey Beach

ATLANTIC OCEAN

REHOBOTH BAY

Delaware State Seashore

Bethany Beach

Fenwick Island

MARYLAND

0   10 Miles

0   10 KM

BEACHES

Sussex County

It defies rationale. Visit Cape Henlopen State Park, Rehoboth, Dewey, Delaware Seashore State Park, Bethany, or Fenwick on a summer day and watch the crazies.

Otherwise sane people bury their friends up to their necks. Some cart truckloads of equipment over burning sand, unload it, sweat and swat flies, yell at their kids for yelling, try to read, give up, pack, and go home. Others balance on glorified toothpicks, waves crashing down on their heads. Many tear into sand-filled sandwiches as if they're pâté de foie gras. Others scan for treasure (or, the odd penny or two). The unlucky are targets for seagulls.

Why do they do it? Are they really crazy? Sure—crazy for the beach! Some things can't be explained. Go see for yourself. Then have your people call my people. I'll be at the beach.

Delaware CURIOSITIES

Buryin' Summer
Bethany Beach

Taking a cue from New Orleans jazz funerals, Bethany Beach residents bid summer adieu with a mock jazz funeral on the boardwalk every Labor Day. A group calling themselves the Friends of Summer sponsors the event, which originated in 1985. It all began when a neighbor of Moss Wagner, who ran the Bethany Beach Ice Cream Parlor in the 1970s and '80s, showed up at Wagner's shop on Labor Day with a bottle of bubbly to mark the bittersweet end of summer. Word spread faster than sand flies. Friends invited friends to the impromptu fest, and next thing you know, it had morphed into an organized event.

Two Dixieland bands lead the procession. Costumed mourner-revelers bear the casket of the departed, a mannequin symbolizing summer, to

the cemetery. In New Orleans, that final resting place would be one of the Crescent City's aboveground cemeteries; in Bethany, it's the boardwalk bandstand. Scores of second-liners follow behind the musicians and pay their respects to the loved one who, with the certainty of the tide, will return to life the following Memorial Day.

And what of Moss Wagner? He gave up the ice-cream business several years ago and moved to Crested Butte, Colorado, where, last we heard, he's a massage therapist.

The deceased return every Memorial Day.

Tower of Power

Cape Henlopen State Park

Weenie-grilling families, surfers off Herring Point, bikers, hikers, and naturalists at peaceful Cape Henlopen State Park (302–645–8983; www.destateparks.com) are sometimes surprised to learn that the imposing concrete towers there are not destination-wedding sites, grain silos, or petrified sand castles. During World War II thirteen towers were erected between Cape May, New Jersey, and Fenwick Island, Delaware, to protect the entrance to Delaware Bay (that is, Wilmington and Philadelphia). They were built to last twenty years, but after sixty years six towers are still intact, some on pilings extending 65 feet below the sand.

Stuck in the tower and not a prince in sight.

In 1964, 543 acres of the Fort Miles base reverted to the State of Delaware and today comprise Cape Henlopen State Park. Visitors can ascend the rebuilt Tower 7, which is 75 feet high with concrete walls 1 foot thick. Here army spotters peered through azimuth range finders and took readings every thirty seconds. Using triangulation (unrelated to strangulation), they phoned the coordinates to commanders manning two 16-inch, two 12-inch, and two 6-inch batteries.

Fortunately, no one had occasion to fire on a German warship. But the threat was very real, and there were some false alarms. The biggest fear was that the *Bismarck* would breach security. If that scenario had played out, a very loud "Oh s@*#!" would have reverberated as far as Wilmington. Maybe Boston. It was no secret that army guns would have been no match for the mighty battle cruiser.

The one with the biggest gun wins.

Beefing up Delaware Bay security, an underwater minefield extended from Cape Henlopen to Cape May, 17 miles away. The mines could be shut off electronically to allow friendly vessels to pass. On a recent tour, I learned that during a beach party after the war, the army decided it'd be fun to blow up the mines. The person in charge pushed button no. 1. Nothing happened. Then he depressed buttons 2, 3, and 4. *Nada. Zilch.* While pondering what might have gone wrong, the soldier got a call from an officer in Cape May who asked, "Why are you blowing up our mines?"

DUNE WHAT COMES NATURALLY

The panoramic view from the top of the Great Dune in Cape Henlopen State Park—of ocean, bay, maritime traffic, Cape May, and beyond—is nothing short of spectacular. At 80 feet above sea level, it is the highest dune between Cape Cod, Massachusetts, and Kitty Hawk, on North Carolina's Outer Banks.

That the Great Dune shifts westward from 3 to 5 feet a year didn't bode well for the Cape Henlopen Lighthouse. Guess the engineers forgot a basic seashore precept: Sand moves. Even with a base 6 feet thick, the lighthouse slid into the ocean in 1926, after guiding ships for more than 150 years. Oops. Rumor has it that after the unfortunate incident *(slip slidin' away . . .)*, locals had a field day, gathering hunks of concrete for Harry Homeowner projects. No word on how the concrete held up.

Doubling Up
Dewey Beach

Consider zip code 19971: a barrier-island sandbox roughly 20 blocks long and 2 blocks wide, snaking north–south between Rehoboth Beach and Delaware Seashore State Park. Signs, T-shirts, bumper stickers, and hats proclaim what local aficionados have long known, without printed reminders: DEWEY BEACH: A WAY OF LIFE.

Boasting a permanent population of approximately 350, between Memorial Day and Labor Day the town swells—like Eddie Murphy in *The Nutty Professor*—to about 30,000. So where do these summer sybarites bed down? Most rental cottages and condos have three or fewer bed-rooms. Dewey motels and hotels number around a dozen, and sleeping on the beach is prohibited.

We can always make room for one more.

Enterprising, cash-strapped twenty-five- to forty-year-olds have found a solution: They get together and rent shares in a house for the season. A house manager handles the finances. For roughly $1,200 to $2,500, one can share a bedroom (bed-sharing is up to the participants) and bath. I've heard that occasional visitors are charged for showering.

As in other humanistic business ventures, there's a sliding scale. Weekdays are cheaper, natch, favoring the self-employed. Nine-to-fivers wait until Friday for the weekly exodus from D.C., Philly, and Baltimore. You do the math. A four-bedroom house with eight single beds yields the owner a nice piece of change. Between June and September, introverts and claustrophobics are better served elsewhere.

Elvis Is in the Building

Dewey Beach

Dewey Beach's annual three-day Elvis Festival draws up to two dozen Elvis impersonators to the Rusty Rudder every September. Contestants from several states come to shake, strum, and strut for the $5,000 first prize.

So dust off your blue suede shoes, slap on a fringed polyester shirt and 48-inch jewel-encrusted belt, and y'all come. What do you have to lose beside your self-respect?

The Rusty Rudder is located in the Ruddertowne complex at 113 Dickinson Street and the Bay. For more information call (302) 227–3888 or go to www.deweybeachlife.com.

BAIT AND SWITCH

Delaware began a two-year moratorium on the commercial harvesting of Delaware Bay horseshoe crabs on January 1, 2007. Why would you give a fig about anything as old and ugly as a horseshoe crab? Because the delicate balance of nature had been upset yet again. And Delaware took a stand to restore that balance.

Local fishermen are pretty crabby about the decision because they historically use cut-up horseshoe crabs to bait their traps for eels and whelks (conch). When that well dries up, bait prices rise. So it's fair to say that they are not happy campers. On the other side, scientists and environmentalists are exchanging high fives because they've been struggling for years to bring about a moratorium. Are they anti-fishing? Mean-spirited? Heck no. They cite the dramatic decline in the horseshoe crab population and also in some migratory birds, especially the red knot. The red knot relies on horseshoe crab eggs for fuel on their annual journey from Tierra del Fuego to the Arctic. If the red knots can't pork out on the eggs along the bay's shores, it's bye-bye, birdie!

Let's hope our kids live to take care of us.

State biologists say the number of bay-feeding red knots has dwindled in recent years—from about 100,000 to 13,000 in 2004. They think disease may have hit the crab population hard, leaving a shortage of eggs and baby crabs—and happy meals for the red knots. The moratorium will allow the crabs two years to lay their eggs without outside interference. Stay tuned.

Gawn to the Dawgs
Dewey Beach

On Columbus Day weekend thousands of greyhounds from all over the country bring their beach chairs, boogie boards, boom boxes, and owners to Dewey Beach for the annual Greyhounds Reach the Beach event (800–446–8637; www.adopt-a-greyhound .org/dewey). It is part fraternity party (for the dogs as much as their caretakers) and part awareness-raising about this sleek, speedy, and gentle breed. Too often they are abandoned and euthanized after they retire from racing. A dog's life? Not always.

Does this bathing suit make me look fat?

Activities at the pooch fest include morning beach walks, an Ice Cream Social (crumbled biscuits on frozen yogurt), canine first aid classes, and a Beer and Biscuit Costume Ball. Many pet-friendly businesses, hotels, and home owners between Lewes and Bethany Beach welcome Fidos and their two-legged chauffeurs. Sharkey's Grill (1508 Highway One, Dewey Beach; 302–226–3116) provides water bowls for the tail-waggers on the restaurant's deck and grass, and owners get complimentary coffee.

If you're thinking of coming, with or without your hound, plan ahead. Rooms are sometimes booked up to a year ahead.

ON THE ROCKS

Can you imagine a state this small with three shipwreck museums in the same county? Well, there are. Before modern navigation, the treacherous shoals off Delaware claimed more mariners, I am told, than the Bermuda Triangle. In fact, 200 known vessels have sunk off Delaware. Maybe that's where the expression "hard rocks" comes from.

Only twice has the state gone in, er, under to preserve wreck sites and collect artifacts: the HM Brig *DeBraak* in 1985 and, more recently, the *Severn*. Not all the artifacts in these museums are from local wrecks; for instance, booty from the *Atocha* figures prominently, too. Count me in with the divers, archeologists, and historians who would like to see a state maritime archaeology program. But please don't ask me to dive—I get claustrophobic in a phone booth.

DiscoverSea Shipwreck Museum (708 Ocean Highway, Fenwick Island; 302–539–9366; www.discoversea.com). About 10,000 artifacts from local and worldwide wrecks are on display at any given time, representing about 20 percent of the collection; the balance is on loan to other museums. (See this chapter's "Booty-ful Treasure" entry.)

Treasures of the Sea (Stephen J. Betze Library, Delaware Technical & Community College, Owens Campus, Route 18, Georgetown; 302–856–5700; www.treasuresofthesea.org). Come here to see treasures from the Spanish galleon *Nuestra Señora de Atocha*. (See "Atocha So" in the Slower Delaware chapter.)

Zwaanendael Museum (102 Kings Highway, Lewes; 302–645–1148; www.history.delaware.gov/museums). Here you'll find artifacts from the *DeBraak,* which went down in a squall off Cape Henlopen in 1798, and the recently discovered *Severn,* which archeologists believe sank in Roosevelt Inlet (Lewes) in 1774. (See this chapter's "Beached" entry.)

Booty-ful Treasure

Fenwick Island

In the DiscoverSea Shipwreck Museum (708 Ocean Highway; 302–539–9366; www.discoversea.com), located over a shell shop, no less, professional diver Dale W. Clifton Jr. cannot shake his booty because it's too heavy. But he sure knows how to dive for it, collect it, and display it.

Take a look at the coins, medical implements, gold jewelry, bullion (no, not the soup), pottery, cannons, and rum bottles (sorry, they're dry). Most date from the mid-sixteenth to mid-nineteenth centuries, and most were scooped—along with prodigious amounts of silt—from shipwrecks off the Delmarva coast. Talk about bling—I wouldn't mind borrowing the 10-foot gold chain from the *Atocha* intended for a queen. (Though the museum is not far from Rehoboth, where there are countless queens, *this* queen was a Spanish monarch, not a cross-dresser.)

Clifton was among the divers who, in 1985, recovered more than $500 million worth of trinkets from the hull of the *Atocha*. The Milton native says treasure diving hooked him in 1980 when he recovered his first coin, a 1775 halfpenny that had belonged to Britain's mad King George III (1760–1820).

Though some 10,000 artifacts are on display at any given time, the *other* 80 percent is on loan to museums worldwide. That's a lot of booty, mon. (*NOTE:* Be sure to check hours before visiting, as they vary depending on season.)

Beached
Lewes Beach

It began in fall 2004 as a ho-hum dredging project of the channel known as Roosevelt Inlet. When completed, about 288,000 tons of sand had been pumped onto Lewes Beach. That might have been the end of the story, except a few months later beach strollers began stepping on more than the usual mussel shells, pop tops, and cigarette butts—stuff like English stoneware, Dutch tobacco pipes, Chinese porcelain, glass, and lead military miniatures. Less than two years later, the Lewes Maritime Archaeology Project had collected approximately 43,000 artifacts—most from locals. Honest folks that they are, they turned in their booty for cleaning, sorting, and labeling.

About the same time, divers located the mostly undisturbed wreck site, about half a mile off Lewes Beach in Delaware Bay. Using digital scanners to pick up the artifacts' sonar images, plus other high-tech tools, they scoured the bottom. By studying the artifacts, assessing the ship's weight and keel size, and examining timbers, anchors, and rigging, members of the archaeological project began piecing together the puzzle. For help in identifying the vessel, they turned to a British researcher who combed insurance-company records of shipwrecks and their cargo lists to find a match.

Subsequent dives in August and September 2006 led to the identification of the vessel as the *Severn,* a 200-ton cargo ship based in Bristol. The vessel went down in Delaware Bay on its way to Philadelphia in May 1774 during a nor'easter. According to Dan Griffith, director of the project, "The *Severn* was a transport, a Wal-Mart and a Home Depot, carrying everything from building materials to toys."

If you're tempted to lend a hand in the recovery effort, be fore-warned: Public access to the wreck is OFF LIMITS. Trespassers face a $20,000 fine and/or thirty days in the slammer. You'd do better to inspect some of the artifacts displayed at the Zwaanendael Museum, 102 Kings Highway at Savannah Road (302–645–1148; www.history .delaware.gov/museums).

Future site of 500 condos and a mall.

BLACKBEARD LOOTED HERE

Avast, mates! Pirates were more than a figment of Robert Louis Stevenson's imagination. In fact, for many years they plied Delaware's waters and made a nice living when things got dull in the West Indies. Predators lying in wait, they patrolled the coast and sailed up Delaware Bay and rivers in the 1600s and 1700s.

The most famous pirate of all, Edward Teach, aka Blackbeard, holed up in Delaware creeks, where he'd catch some z's and repair sails before raiding poor unsuspecting blokes. Though unsubstantiated, because pirates seldom leave calling cards, the word on the water is that pirates sacked Lewes in 1698. Supposedly, Teach's sword, inscribed with "bb," was found in Blackbird Creek in the Blackbird State Forest (formerly Blackbeard Creek) in southern New Castle County.

Though the Brits did their best to clear the area of pirates in the late eighteenth century, they failed to take out the land pirates. These "moon cussers," whose work required darkness, would burn large beach fires that resembled lighthouses from the water. Clever, no? Grog-filled mariners, their judgment impaired, took the bait, mistook the fires for lighthouses, and ran aground, where the moon cussers waited to loot.

Locals who keep track of such things say the moon cussers' descendants still live in the area. My lips are sealed. But I believe I've spotted more than a few at local watering holes, especially during happy hour. Arrr!

Have backscratcher, will travel.

A Ferry Nice Ride

Lewes

When the Chesapeake Bay Bridge-Tunnel opened in April 1964, joining Cape Charles, Maryland, and Hampton Roads, Virginia, at the southern end of Chesapeake Bay, a quandary arose: What do you do with four obsolete vessels? Drag them to Goodwill? Float them in the backyard pool?

Getting there really is half the fun.

Well, it just so happens the Cape May–Lewes Ferry (800–64–FERRY; www.capemaylewesferry.com) was in the market for vessels. The secondhand boats were put into service for the ferry's maiden voyage in July 1964. Talk about synchronicity.

A decade later they added new vessels to the fleet and retired the old ones to Davy Jones's locker. With the 1990s came major renovations, like cushy interior seating and air-conditioning, and the addition to the larger vessels of a food court, bars, and an elevator—very convenient if you've tipped a few. One misstep and find out the meaning of "hit the deck."

While the ferry service was created as a transportation link, it has become an attraction unto itself. You may recall years ago when the airline industry advertised "Getting there is half the fun." Today flying is less than one-sixteenth of the fun, if it's any fun at all. That concept has been jettisoned to the attic along with Nehru jackets and penny candy. Not so for the ferry experience. Many folks detour from the straight and paved and are more than willing to increase their travel time to experience the ride. It sure beats putting up with traffic and roadwork. Besides, you can't glimpse dolphins and ospreys, breathe fumeless air, or sip a brewski while driving on Interstate 95. At least, I hope not.

Blacktop Graveyard
Lewes

The next time you park in the lot adjacent to the Lewes terminal of the Cape May–Lewes Ferry on Cape Henlopen Drive, pause a moment and pay your respects to the 800 or so dead buried beneath your sports car or SUV. Say what? The tract was known as the Unknown Sailor's Grave-yard until developers earmarked it as a parking lot necessity in the 1960s. Rather than move the remains of the largely forgotten mariners, they paved over them. One would assume that this, um, sealed the sailors' fate once and for all, but apparently not. Some of their spirits have been spotted roaming the premises on numerous occasions.

In interviews for his books on East Coast paranormal experiences, author Ed Okonowicz spoke to several workers who reported sightings in and around the terminal. Look around while you're killing time before boarding the ferry. Those restless souls may be waiting their turns at the putt-putt course, shopping for souvenir sweatshirts, or getting a cup of coffee and hot dog to go.

Back in the 1990s a college student on the night shift in the police administration building reported "black mist rising from the computer and copy machines" that took on "something like a shape of a figure." And, no, his PC hadn't crashed, nor had he ingested the other kind (the one with the second "P"). A cleaning woman, also on the graveyard shift, said her radio went bananas. The stations and volume changed repeatedly, for no good reason. Once, she said, she "felt a full hand" on her shoulder.

If you have a minute, check out the memorial marker behind the gift shop. The last line reads, "May they find eternal repose." It doesn't sound like they have.

Happy Birthday to Lew

Lewes

The first town in the First State celebrated its 375th birthday in grand style September 15–17, 2006. Visitors toured Delaware's tall ship and goodwill ambassador, the *Kalmar Nyckel,* and three other tall ships docked in town for the festivities. With reverence for (and apologies to) serious historians, here's a watered-down take on the town's colorful history.

Henry Hudson, out for a sail one day in 1609, was the first to "discover" the area. But he didn't stay, citing pressing business farther north. Or, as some muse, no slips were available at the town's marinas, it being a holiday weekend. About twenty years later some savvy Dutch investors arrived, chanting real estate's mantra—*Location, location, location!* They knew in a heartbeat that whaling the converging waters of the Atlantic Ocean and Delaware Bay would turn a *whale* of a profit.

You want me to climb up what?

At first the real original settlers did not welcome the newbies with open arms, if you get my drift. In fact, the *Bloody* Mary (preferably made with Old Bay seasoning) may have originated here. British courts later ceded the land to William Penn (you remember Bill—nice looking, good student, loved to travel), and it was called Lewes, after a town in Sussex County, England.

In subsequent years the residents put up with piracy, shipwrecks, and the War of 1812, during which a British frigate fired on the town, killing a hen. Visit the Cannonball House (built circa 1765) at 118 Front Street. As the name suggests, you can see the cannonball protruding from the house.

Call (302) 645–7670 or visit www.historiclewes.org for more information.

Jazzy Bouquet

Lewes

They said it couldn't be done, that you couldn't grow grapes in Delaware. But Peggy Raley—an accomplished jazz singer—wasn't buying it. After writing about wine for several years, Peggy decided to give winemaking a try; however, a small impediment blocked her dream. State law said you couldn't grow grapes for wine. Not one to take no for an answer, a very determined Peggy went to the state and got a farm winery law passed.

In 1987 she opened Nassau Valley Vineyards, Delaware's first and only winery, with her dad on the family farm (32165 Winery Way; 302–645–9463; www.nassauvalley.com). Like fine wine, it took time and

TLC. To those naysayers who said grapes would not flourish in southern Delaware, Peggy says the maritime climate and soil are ideal for growing difficult grapes for wines such as Cabernet Sauvignon. But don't take my word for it . . .

And they said grapes wouldn't grow here.

Plankety-Plank

Lewes

Tom Thumb would have been comfortable in the Lilliputian-size Early Plank House—but he wouldn't have been able to entertain. This "house" is so small, you have to go outside to change your mind. Historians say that the home, one of the town's earliest structures, housed Scandinavian settlers (plural!) in the early 1700s. One thing's for sure: There's no room for a smorgasbord. (Maybe a Swedish meatball or two . . .)

One of a dozen buildings overseen by the Lewes Historical Society, it's a typical one-room cabin with a wooden floor and hand-carved clothes pegs—and not a DVD player or plasma screen in sight. The cabin once stood on nearby Pilottown Road before it was restored and moved here in 1963. I'll bet a strapping local carried it under his arm along with a quart of milk and the *Cape Gazette*.

The Plank House is located at 110 Ship Carpenter Street at Third Street. Call (302) 645–7670 or go to www.historiclewes.org for more information.

Cozy fixer-upper in a great location.

Weighty News
Lewes

Do we need the American Obesity Association to tell us that 9 million Americans are severely or morbidly obese? Look around. Little kids are no longer little. Teens resemble linebackers. On airplanes, adults spill into their neighbor's seats—or laps. The sobering news, according to the association: About 60 million of us are obese. The Center for Disease Control and Prevention says that those 20 and older weigh on average 24 pounds more than the same age group did 40 years ago.

Well, Delaware is doing its part. Delaware may be the second smallest state geographically but it's at the forefront in the nation's *weighty* problem. In fact, the state is the 29th heaviest, and "one of 31 states where obesity rates rose" between 2005 and 2006, says a Trust for America's Health report. Delaware has an obesity rate of 22.8 percent of the adult population—that's nearly 23 of every 100 First Staters. C'mon folks. Do you really need that third helping of fried chicken?

Rather than stressing abstinence and exercise, the prevailing philosophy seems to be, if you can't beat 'em, join 'em. And hospitals are among those going with the flow in this ever-*growing* problem. Beebe Medical Center in Lewes, like many hospitals across the country, stocks hospital gowns up to XXXXL. Excuse me. I thought that was the date of an important Roman battle, not a garment size.

An analyst for a major R & D company estimates that sales of bariatric products (larger beds, surgical tables, scales, and larger instruments to accommodate those tipping the scale at 300 pounds or more) will top $1 billion in 2011. I'm definitely in the wrong field.

Disney East
Rehoboth Beach

A bevy of Disney lawyers, witnesses, and defendants packed the chichi Bellmoor Inn (6 Christian Street; 302–227–5800; www.thebellmoor .com) in Rehoboth Beach in late fall 2004 and again in January 2005. No, they weren't there for a sand castle contest, or to plan a new theme park.

What lured them to the usually low-key, family-friendly town was a trial in Delaware's Court of Chancery in nearby Georgetown, 16 miles west of the french fries and caramel corn. In a class-action suit, Walt Disney Company shareholders took the board of directors to task. Seems they were ticked off that that the company paid a $140 million severance package to Michael Ovitz when Disney showed him the door in 1996. Of course, the court upheld Disney. That's Fantasyland for ya.

A favorite of well-heeled visitors, corporate and otherwise, the family-owned Bellmoor's guest book read like a who's who of the rich and famous when the Disney team departed. Roy and Patty Disney, Michael and Jane Eisner, Michael Ovitz, and Sidney Poitier (plus their attorneys and support staff), in addition to *Vanity Fair* celeb journalist Dominick Dunne and reporters from major dailies between Wilmington and LA, left their John Hancocks.

Between courthouse sessions, the guests enjoyed the Bellmoor's fifty rooms and suites—some with fireplaces, hydrotherapy tubs, and kitchens. Stressed from the trials of the trial, the Disney crew unwound in the fitness center and spa, and got stoned with a certified massage therapist (that's hot stone therapy, not the other kind). I understand that in addition to tucking in hospital corners and fetching extra towels, the helpful staff also filled orders at a local health food store for Ovitz's protein shakes. Yes, friends, all is possible in the Magic Kingdom.

We should relocate. This is much nicer than Burbank.

INDEX

INDEX

INDEX

INDEX

INDEX

INDEX

About the Author

The first twenty years of her life, Beth Rubin knew Delaware as a pit stop between Washington, D.C., and New Jersey. Every time she passed through, she wondered what Delaware would be like if she gave it more than three minutes. Soon after moving to Maryland in the early 1960s, she had her chance. She went to Rehoboth Beach one day. She was hooked. On nice days her kids would come home to an empty house and a note: I'LL BE BACK WHEN IT RAINS. FEED YOUR FATHER AND THE DOG.

At every opportunity Beth still crosses the Maryland border—unfenced and, as yet, unpatrolled—to wiggle her toes in the sands of Delaware's pristine beaches. She's branched out over the past forty-plus years to explore every corner of the state. Sometimes she feels like Thelma and Louise. To maintain her stamina on the road, she fuels up with some of the best seafood, barbecue, chicken, pizza, and subs on the planet while satisfying the basic food groups (fat, salt, bulk).

Beth has won awards for novel-length fiction and travel books. When not burning rubber, she writes features, essays, and humor—for anyone who pays within thirty days—from her home/office in Annapolis, Maryland.